W9-CAL-135

Spelling Skills

Grade 2

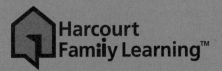

Harcourt
Family Learning™

Copyright © 2005 by Spark Educational Publishing
Adapted from *Steck-Vaughn Spelling: Linking Words to Meaning, Level 2*
by John R. Pescosolido
Copyright © 2002 by Harcourt Achieve
Licensed under special arrangement with Harcourt Achieve.

Flash Kids is a trademark of SparkNotes LLC.
Harcourt Family Learning and Design is a trademark of Harcourt, Inc.
All rights reserved. No part of this book may be used or reproduced in
any manner whatsoever without the written permission of the Publisher.

ISBN 1-4114-0383-5

Please submit changes or report errors to *www.sparknotes.com/errors*
For more information, please visit *www.flashkidsbooks.com*

Printed and bound in China

Spark Educational Publishing
A Division of Barnes & Noble Publishing
120 Fifth Avenue
New York, NY 10011

Dear Parent,

As your child learns to read and write, he or she is bound to discover that the English language contains very many words, and that no single set of rules is used to spell all of these words. This can feel rather confusing and overwhelming for a young reader. But by completing the fun, straightforward activities in this workbook, your child will practice spelling the words that he or she is most likely to encounter in both classroom and everyday reading. To make the path to proper spelling even easier, each lesson presents second-grade words in lists grouped by vowel sound, suffix, or related forms, like plurals and contractions. This order will clearly show your child the different ways that similar sounds can be spelled.

Each of the 30 lessons begins by asking your child to say each word in the word list. This exercise helps him or her to make the connection between a word's appearance and what it sounds like. Next, he or she will sort the words, which teaches the relationship between a sound and its spelling patterns. Your child will then encounter a variety of activities that will strengthen his or her understanding of the meaning and use of each word. These include recognizing definitions, synonyms, and base words, as well as using capitalization and punctuation. Be sure to have a children's or adult dictionary available, which your child will need to use for some of the exercises. Each lesson also features a short passage containing spelling and grammar mistakes that your child will proofread and correct, using the proofreading marks on page 7. Once he or she can recognize both correct and incorrect spellings, your child is ready for the next lesson!

Throughout this workbook are brief unit reviews to help reinforce knowledge of the words that have been learned in the lessons. Your child can use the answer key to check his or her work in the lessons and reviews. Also, take advantage of everyday opportunities to improve spelling skills. By asking your child to read stories or newspaper articles to you at home, or billboards and signs while traveling, you are showing your child how often he or she will encounter these words. You can also give your child extra practice in writing these correct spellings by having him or her write a shopping list or note to a family member.

Since learning to spell can be frustrating, your child may wish to use one or more of the spelling strategies on page 6 when he or she finds a word or group of words difficult to master. You can also encourage your child to use the following study steps to learn a word:

1. Say the word. What consonant sounds do you hear? What vowel sounds do you hear? How many syllables do you hear?

2. Look at the letters in the word. Think about how each sound is spelled. Find any spelling patterns or parts that you know. Close your eyes. Picture the word in your mind.

3. Spell the word aloud.

4. Write the word. Say each letter as you write it.

5. Check the spelling. If you did not spell the word correctly, use the study steps again.

With help from you and this workbook, your child is well on the way to excellent skills in spelling, reading, and writing!

Table of contents

spelling strategies

What can you do when you aren't sure how to spell a word?

Say the word aloud. Make sure you say it correctly. Listen to the sounds in the word. Think about letters and patterns that might spell the sounds.

Look in the Spelling Table on page 141 to find common spellings for sounds in the word.

Think about related words. They may help you spell the word you're not sure of.

longer—long

Guess the spelling of the word and check it in a dictionary.

Write the word in different ways. Compare the spellings and choose the one that looks correct.

tyger   tieger
(tiger)   tigher

Draw the shape of the word to help you remember its spelling.

Choose a rhyming helper and use it. A rhyming helper is a word that rhymes with the word and is spelled like it.

fell—bell

Create a memory clue to help you remember the spelling.

<u>Cold</u> has the word <u>old</u>.

Proofreading Marks

Mark	Meaning	Example
⬭	spell correctly	I (liek) dogs.
⊙	add period	They are my favorite kind of pet⊙
?	add question mark	What kind of pet do you have?
≡	capitalize	My dog's name is scooter
¶	indent paragraph	¶Scooter is my best friend. He wakes me up every morning. He sleeps with me every night. He plays with me all the time.
⌄ ⌄	add quotation marks	"You are a good dog," I tell him.

Words with Short a

van	an	after	flat	hand	cat
and	has	am	than	add	man

Say and Listen

Say each spelling word. Listen for the vowel sound you hear in van.

cat

Think and Sort

The vowel sound in van is called short a. All of the spelling words have the short a sound. It is spelled a. Spell each word aloud.

Look at the letters in each word. Is the short a at the beginning or in the middle of the word?

1. Write the **five** spelling words that have short a at the beginning, like add.

2. Write the **seven** spelling words that have short a in the middle, like van.

1. Beginning Short a

_____ _____

_____ _____

_____

2. Middle Short a

_____ _____

_____ _____

_____ _____

_____

Clues

Write the spelling word for each clue.

1. pet that meows _____

2. part of an arm _____

3. what you can do with numbers _____

4. the opposite of **before** _____

5. what a boy grows up to be _____

Letter Scramble

Unscramble the letters in dark type to make a spelling word. Write the word to complete the sentence.

6. na   I ate _____ apple.

7. hant   His friend is older _____ he is.

8. ahs   Rita is not here because she _____ a cold.

9. ma   You are tall, but I _____ short.

10. latf   The top of a table is _____.

11. dna   Sam likes blue _____ purple.

van	an	after	flat	hand	cat
and	has	am	than	add	man

Proofreading

Proofread the report below. Use these proofreading marks to correct four spelling mistakes, one capitalization mistake, and one punctuation mistake. See the chart on page 7 to learn how to use the proofreading marks.

Proofreading Marks

◯ spell correctly
≡ capitalize
⊙ add period

Science Field Trip   Monday, October 3

1. Where did you go?

we went to Lance Wildlife Park.

2. What did you see?

A mann held a baby bottle in his handd.

He fed a baby tiger We saw ane alligator swim.

3. What did you like best?

I liked the elephant best. I amm glad we went.

Language Connection

Capital Letters

Use a capital letter to begin the first word of a sentence.

> **My** cat climbs trees all the time.

Choose the correct word in dark type to complete each sentence. Then write the sentence correctly. Remember to begin the sentence with a capital letter.

1. my (**cat**, **and**) is stuck in a tree.

_____

2. a (**flat**, **man**) comes to help.

_____

3. he (**hand**, **has**) a ladder.

_____

4. she jumps down (**after**, **and**) runs home.

_____

More Words with Short a

catch   fast   matter   have   land   that
back   last   thank   ask   sang   black

catch

Say and Listen

Say each spelling word. Listen for the short a sound.

Think and Sort

All of the spelling words have the short a sound. It is spelled a. Spell each word aloud.

Look at the letters in each spelling word. Is the short a at the beginning or in the middle of the word?

1. Write the **one** word that has short a at the beginning.

2. Write the **eleven** words that have short a in the middle, like back, and fast. One word has an e at the end, but the e is silent. Circle the word.

1. Beginning Short a
_____

2. Middle Short a
_____   _____

_____   _____

_____   _____

_____   _____

_____

Word Groups

Write the spelling word that belongs in each group.

1. danced, acted, _____

2. sea, sky, _____

3. orange, yellow, _____

4. throw, hit, _____

5. quick, swift, _____

6. had, has, _____

Rhymes

Write the spelling word that completes each
sentence and rhymes with the underlined word.

7. Why did Dee _____ for that silly <u>mask</u>?

8. Hector wanted to _____ me for the piggy <u>bank</u>.

9. What is the _____ with the pancake <u>batter</u>?

10. Ming ran around the <u>track</u> and _____ home.

11. What is the name of _____ <u>cat</u>?

catch	fast	matter	have	land	that
back	last	thank	ask	sang	black

Proofreading

Proofread the letter below. Use proofreading marks to correct four spelling mistakes, one capitalization mistake, and one punctuation mistake.

Proofreading Marks
◯ spell correctly
≡ capitalize
⊙ add period

Sidney,

Do you know where I can cach bus 145? Thet bus will take me to my piano lesson. I love to play. Laste week I learned a new song. my teacher will aske me to play it Maybe I will play it for you, too.

Max

Periods

Use a period at the end of a sentence that tells something.

Camels live in the desert.

Choose the word from the sun below that completes each sentence. Then write the sentence correctly. Remember to put a period at the end.

fast   **back**   **land**   **have**

1. A camel can carry people on its _____

_____

2. Some camels _____ one hump

_____

3. Camels can run _____

_____

4. They run across dry _____

_____

Words with Short e

| ten | when | bed | shelf | jet | yes |
| said | went | kept | says | next | end |

bed

Say and Listen

Say each spelling word. Listen for
the vowel sound you hear in ten.

Think and Sort

The vowel sound in bed is called short e.
All of the spelling words have the short e sound.
Spell each word aloud.

Look at the letters in each word. Think about how short e is spelled.

1. Write the **ten** spelling words that have short e spelled e, like ten.

2. Write the **one** spelling word that has short e spelled ay.

3. Write the **one** spelling word that has short e spelled ai.

1. e Words

_____   _____

_____   _____

_____   _____

_____   _____

_____   _____

2. ay Word   **3. ai Word**

_____   _____

Word Math

Add and subtract letters and picture names. Write each spelling word.

1. b +  − sl = _____

2. sh + _____ = _____

3. w + _____ = _____

4. _____ − am + et = _____

5. _____ − p + d = _____

Word Groups

Write the spelling word that belongs in each group.

6. near, beside, _____

7. told, asked, _____

8. saved, stored, _____

9. eight, nine, _____

10. no, maybe, _____

11. tells, asks, _____

ten	when	bed	shelf	jet	yes
said	went	kept	says	next	end

Proofreading

Proofread the postcard below. Use proofreading marks to correct four spelling mistakes, one capitalization mistake, and one punctuation mistake.

Proofreading Marks

⬯ spell correctly
☰ capitalize
⊙ add period

Dear Lan,

We wint on a train trip When the train turned a big corner, we saw the train car at the very ende! I slept in the top bed. ted slept in the bottom one. He sayd the sounds kept him awake. I slept great. I want you to come with us naxt time.

Love, Fern

Lan Chin

12 Ventura Dr.

Cleveland, OH

44108

Sentences

A sentence begins with a capital letter and ends with a period or other end mark. Unscramble each sentence and write it correctly.

1. ten cats my friend has

_____

2. hid they under the bed

_____

3. on a shelf they sat

_____

4. they toy played mouse with a

_____

More Words with Short e

best	well	any	seven	many	dress
desk	rest	bell	send	help	egg

bell

Say and Listen

Say each spelling word. Listen for the short e sound.

Think and Sort

Look at the letters in each word. Think about how short e is spelled. How many spellings for short e do you see?

1. Write the **ten** spelling words that have short e spelled e, like desk.

2. Write the **two** spelling words that have short e spelled a, like any.

1. e Words

_____   _____

_____   _____

_____   _____

_____   _____

_____

2. a Words

_____   _____

Word Groups

Write the spelling word that belongs in each group.

1. five, six, _____

2. several, lots, _____

3. table, chair, _____

4. good, better, _____

5. one, every, _____

6. good, fine, _____

What's Missing?

Write the missing spelling word.

7. the chicken and the _____

8. ring the _____

9. _____ an e-mail

10. _____ when you're tired

11. a woman's _____

best	well	any	seven	many	dress
desk	rest	bell	send	help	egg

Proofreading

Proofread the diary page below.
Use proofreading marks to
correct four spelling mistakes,
one capitalization mistake, and
one punctuation mistake.

Proofreading Marks

◯ spell correctly

≡ capitalize

? add question mark

Dear Diary,

What will I do with so meny baby turtles

Grandfather can take sevan. Riley says she

does not want eny. I asked Mom if I could

keep just one. that is the bist idea. She says I

can. I will take good care of my baby turtle.

That's all for today.

Dictionary Skills

Using the Spelling Table

A spelling table can help you find a word in a dictionary. It shows different spellings for a sound. Suppose you are not sure how to spell the last sound in **pick**. Is it **c**, **k**, **ch**, or **ck**? First, find the sound and the example words in the table. Then read the first spelling for the sound and look up **pic** in a dictionary. Look for each spelling in the dictionary until you find the correct one.

Sound	Example Words	Spellings
k	can, keep, school, sick	c k ch ck

Use the Spelling Table on page 141 and a dictionary to write the missing letters in the picture names.

1.  _____ ity

2.  bla _____

3.  _____ ale

4.  s _____ool

5.  mou _____ e

6.  sn _____ l

People Words

had	class	him	you	children	boys
our	girls	the	them	her	child

Say and Listen

Say the spelling words. Listen to the sounds in each word.

girls

Think and Sort

Look at the letters in each word. Think about how each sound in the word is spelled. Spell each word aloud.

1. Write the **six** spelling words that have three letters, like him.

2. Write the **six** spelling words that have more than three letters, like boys.

1. Three Letters

_____   _____

_____   _____

_____   _____

2. More Than Three Letters

_____   _____

_____   _____

_____   _____

Letter Scramble

Unscramble the letters in dark type to make a spelling word. Write the word to complete the sentence.

1. **hmet**   The lions have their cubs with _____.

2. **reh**   That is _____ new dress.

3. **hte**   I saw a baby bird at _____ park.

4. **lascs**   My _____ went to the zoo.

5. **cdlnerhi**   Young people are called _____.

6. **lihdc**   The little _____ had a toy boat.

7. **rou**   Four people will fit in _____ car.

Rhymes

Write the spelling word that completes each sentence and rhymes with the underlined word.

8. Do you know what <u>Dad</u> _____?

9. Those two _____ have lots of <u>toys</u>.

10. Happy birthday <u>to</u> _____!

11. Did you see _____ <u>swim</u>?

| had | class | him | you | children | boys |
| our | girls | the | them | her | child |

Proofreading

Proofread the journal page below. Use proofreading marks to correct four spelling mistakes, one capitalization mistake, and one punctuation mistake.

Proofreading Marks

⬭ spell correctly
☰ capitalize
⊙ add period

September 2

    Today was my first day at Pine School. I had fun. My clas has twenty childrin. There are three new gurls, counting me

    I played tag with Ellie and Adam at recess. when the bell rang, I knew I had made new friends. Owr teacher seems nice, too!

Dictionary Skills

ABC Order

Look at a dictionary. The first word begins with an **a**. The last word begins with a **z**. The words in a dictionary are in ABC order. This order is also called alphabetical order.

Write the missing letters in the alphabet.

a _ c d _ f _ _ i j k _ m

n _ p q _ _ t u v _ x y _

Write these words in alphabetical order.

1. _____

2. _____

3. _____

4. _____

5. _____

6. _____

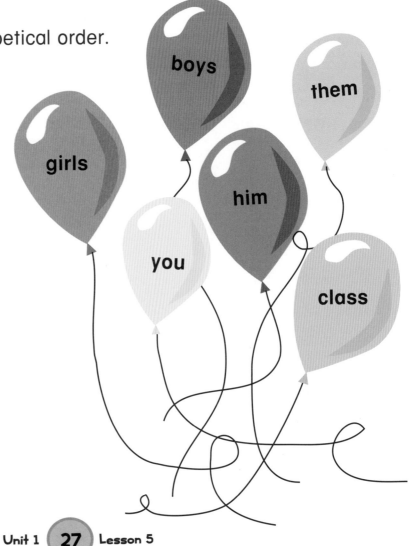

unit 1 Review
Lessons 1-5

Lesson **1**

am

after

than

hand

Words with Short a

Write the spelling word that completes each sentence.

1. Look at the shell in my _____.

2. I _____ going to have strawberry jam.

3. What did they want to do _____ the show?

4. I ran faster _____ James did.

Lesson **2**

ask

have

catch

that

More Words with Short a

Unscramble the letters in dark type to make a spelling word. Then write the word to complete the sentence.

5. **hatt**   Is _____ your puppy?

6. **ska**   Let's _____ them to come with us.

7. **avhe**   Did you _____ fun at the pool?

8. **tchac**   I can _____ a football.

Words with Short e

kept
when
says
said

Write the spelling word for each definition.

9. speaks _____

10. stored _____

11. at what time _____

12. talked _____

More Words with Short e

seven
egg
many
any

Write the spelling word for each clue.

13. This is what a baby bird comes from.

_____

14. You have this when you have a lot of things. _____

15. This is one of several. _____

16. Four and three make this. _____

People Words

our
you
girls
children

Write the missing spelling word.

17. a cake for me and _____

18. games for boys and _____

19. mothers and their _____

20. your team and _____ team

Words with Short i

big	will	fill	this	pick	hid
ship	six	hill	wind	his	trick

ship

Say and Listen

Say each spelling word. Listen for the vowel sound you hear in big.

Think and Sort

The vowel sound you hear in big is called short i. All the spelling words have the short i sound. Spell each word aloud.

Look at the letters in each word. Think about how short i is spelled.

1. Write the **four** spelling words that have three letters.

2. Write the **seven** spelling words that have four letters.

3. Write the **one** spelling word that has five letters.

---

1. Three Letters

_____   _____

_____   _____

2. Four Letters

_____   _____

_____   _____

_____   _____

_____

3. Five Letters _____

Clues

Write the spelling word for each clue.

1. something you can climb   _____

2. a big boat   _____

3. to play a joke on someone   _____

4. the number after five   _____

5. what makes a kite fly   _____

Rhymes

Write the spelling word that completes each sentence and rhymes with the underlined word.

6. <u>Jill</u>, please _____ my glass with water.

7. Luis said that _____ hat <u>is</u> lost.

8. That <u>wig</u> is too _____ for my head.

9. <u>Mick</u> will _____ an apple from that tree.

10. I will <u>miss</u> riding _____ pony.

11. Marco _____ <u>still</u> be here tomorrow.

big	will	fill	this	pick	hid
ship	six	hill	wind	his	trick

Proofreading

Proofread the letter below. Use proofreading marks to correct four spelling mistakes, one capitalization mistake, and one punctuation mistake.

Proofreading Marks

◯ spell correctly
≡ capitalize
⊙ add period

Hi, Jason!

    I just got a new model ship. Now I have sixe

If I had to pik my favorite one, it would be the

sailing ship. it is very big. The sails really work, too.

When the winde hits them, they fil with air. The

ship looks great sailing on the water! What is

your favorite kind of ship?

                      Ryan

Question Marks

Use a question mark at the end of a sentence that asks a question.

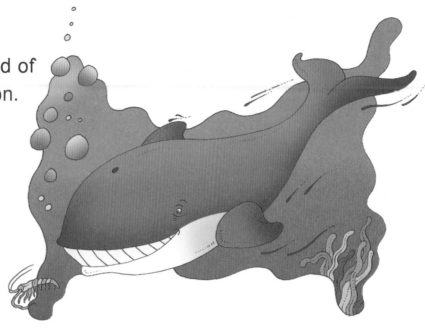

> What is the biggest animal in the world?
> Where is it found?

Choose the correct word in dark type to complete each question. Then write the question correctly. Remember to end it with a question mark.

1. How (**big**, **pick**) is a blue whale

_____

2. Is it as large as a (**ship**, **six**)

_____

3. What does (**this**, **trick**) animal eat

_____

4. Can you see (**hid**, **his**) tail

_____

More Words with Short i

ring	fish	thing	spring	live	swim
give	think	wish	with	sister	bring

Say and Listen

Say each spelling word. Listen for the short i sound.

fish

Think and Sort

All of the spelling words have the short i sound. Spell each word aloud.

Look at the letters in each word. Think about how short i is spelled.

1. Write the **seven** spelling words that have four letters. Two of the words with four letters have an e at the end, but the e is silent. Circle these words.

2. Write the **three** spelling words that have five letters.

3. Write the **two** spelling words that have six letters.

---

1. Four Letters

_____   _____

_____   _____

_____   _____

_____

2. Five Letters

_____   _____

_____

3. Six Letters

_____   _____

Rhymes

Write the spelling word that completes each sentence and rhymes with the underlined word.

1. Birds <u>sing</u> in the _____ .

2. The fried _____ was on the <u>dish</u>.

3. The <u>king</u> wore a shiny gold _____ .

4. I _____ Ben is at the skating <u>rink</u>.

5. Please _____ us some <u>string</u> for the kite.

Word Meaning

Write the spelling word for each meaning. Use a dictionary if you need to.

6. to hope for something _____

7. to hand something over _____

8. a girl with the same parents as another child _____

9. an object _____

10. to move through water _____

11. having _____

ring	fish	thing	spring	live	swim
give	think	wish	with	sister	bring

Proofreading

Proofread this paragraph from a newspaper article. Use proofreading marks to correct four spelling mistakes, one capitalization mistake, and one punctuation mistake.

Proofreading Marks

◯ spell correctly

≡ capitalize

? add question mark

It is time to plant gardens! First, thnk about what you want to plant. Do you want to grow flowers or vegetables Then head out to your yard. Brang your shovel witt you. it is the best thinge for getting the soil ready for seeds.

Vegetables
Finest Quality Seeds

Flowers
Finest Quality Seeds

Dictionary Skills

ABC Order

When two words begin with the same letter, use the second letter to put the words in alphabetical order. Look at the words in the box. **Bell** comes before **big** because **e** comes before **i** in the alphabet.

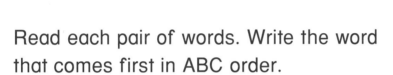

Bell	Big

Read each pair of words. Write the word that comes first in ABC order.

1. swim, sister _____

2. got, give _____

3. ring, run _____

4. luck, live _____

5. spring, stick _____

6. thing, trick _____

7. woman, wish _____

Words with Short o

| hot | dot | block | job | top | hop |
| what | not | was | jog | on | got |

block

Say and Listen

Say each spelling word. Listen for the vowel sound you hear in hot.

Think and Sort

The vowel sound you hear in hot is called short o. All the spelling words have the short o sound. Spell each word aloud.

Look at the letters in each word. Think about how short o is spelled. How many spellings for short o do you see?

1. Write the **ten** spelling words that have short o spelled o, like dot.

2. Write the **two** spelling words that have short o spelled a, like was.

1. o Words

_____   _____

_____   _____

_____   _____

_____   _____

_____   _____

2. a Words

_____   _____

Word Groups

Write the spelling word that belongs in each group.

1. run, trot, _____

2. cold, warm, _____

3. skip, jump, _____

4. spot, mark, _____

5. work, chore, _____

6. town, street, _____

7. took, grabbed, _____

Presto Change-O

Change the order of each word in dark type
to make a spelling word. Write the spelling word
to complete the sentence.

8. no   Please turn _____ the light.

9. ton   Do _____ touch the oven!

10. tahw   Please tell me _____ this is.

11. saw   Who _____ at the door?

Proofreading

Proofread the sign below. Use proofreading marks to correct four spelling mistakes, one capitalization mistake, and one punctuation mistake.

Proofreading Marks
- ◯ spell correctly
- ≡ capitalize
- ⊙ add period

Jason's Pet Care

do you have a cat or a dog? I can care for it when you are nat home My name is Jason White. I live un this blok. My phone number is 555-4100. Call and tell me wat you need. I will give you a good price. I will also take great care of your pet.

Capital Letters

Use a capital letter for the word **I** and to begin the names of people and pets.

Choose the correct word in dark type to complete each sentence. Then write the sentence. Remember to use capital letters.

1. corey jones wanted to go for a (**jog**, **got**).

_____

2. He and i ran around the (**block**, **dot**).

_____

3. i saw rusty (**top**, **hop**) on the porch.

_____

4. She (**not**, **got**) the paper.

_____

5. rusty (**was**, **what**) running fast.

_____

More Words with Short o

box	rock	want	clock	chop	pond
wash	spot	drop	stop	ox	shop

pond

Say and Listen

Say each spelling word. Listen for the short o sound.

Think and Sort

All of the spelling words have the short o sound. Spell each word aloud.

Look at the letters in each word. Think about how short o is spelled. How many spellings for short o do you see?

1. Write the **ten** spelling words that have short o spelled o, like shop.

2. Write the **two** spelling words that have short o spelled a, like want.

1. o Words

_____   _____

_____   _____

_____   _____

_____   _____

_____   _____

2. a Words

_____   _____

Word Groups

Write the spelling word that belongs in each group.

1. time, watch, _____

2. wish, need, _____

3. wait, quit, _____

4. cut, slice, _____

5. cow, horse, _____

6. ocean, lake, _____

7. clean, scrub, _____

More Than One Meaning

Some words have more than one meaning. Complete each pair of sentences with the correct spelling word.

8. We like to _____ at that store.

   I buy my skates at a sports _____.

9. There's a dirty _____ on my dress.

   Put the book in that _____.

10. I just felt a _____ of rain.

    That glass will break if you _____ it.

11. I found this _____ in my back yard.

    Will you _____ the baby?

| box | rock | want | clock | chop | pond |
| wash | spot | drop | stop | ox | shop |

Proofreading

Proofread the note below. Use proofreading marks to correct four spelling mistakes, one capitalization mistake, and one punctuation mistake.

Proofreading Marks

⊙ spell correctly

≡ capitalize

? add question mark

Mom,

Can we go shopping at the new

supermarket today? We need some

soap to wosh our hands. i would like a

bax of cereal. Can I have the kind with

nuts Maybe we can shopp for a new

clok, too. Dad says he wants one with

big numbers.

milk
eggs
bread
fruit
soup

Word Meanings

The dictionary entry for a word gives its meaning.

ox *plural* **oxen.** A male animal of the cattle family. *A strong ox is a useful farm animal.*

⟵ **meaning**

Write the word from the box below that names each picture. Then find each word in a dictionary. Complete the meaning for the word.

pond   ox   spot   rock

Word		**Meaning**
1. _____		a male animal of the _____ family
2. _____		a small body of _____
3. _____		a _____ mark
4. _____		_____ stone

Plural Words

men	eggs	vans	hands	jets	desks
dresses	ships	cats	jobs	bells	backs

Say and Listen

Say the spelling words.
Listen to the ending sounds.

cats

Think and Sort

All of the spelling words are plural words.
Plural words name more than one thing. Spell each word aloud.

Most plural words end in s or es. Look at the letters in each word.

1. Write the **ten** words that end in s, like hands.

2. Write the **one** word that ends in es.

3. Write the **one** word that does not end in s or es.

1. Plural with **s**

_____   _____

_____   _____

_____   _____

_____   _____

_____   _____

2. Plural with **es**   **3.** Other Plural

_____   _____

Clues

Write the spelling word for each clue.

1. what women wear _____

2. things to ring _____

3. big boats _____

4. what chickens lay _____

Letter Scramble

Unscramble the letters in dark type to make a spelling word. Write the word to complete the sentence.

5. **navs**   The school _____ have ten seats.

6. **bosj**   Both my brothers have _____.

7. **cabks**   These chairs have tall _____.

8. **nem**   Those _____ are my uncles.

9. **shand**   My _____ are in my pockets.

10. **tejs**   Two _____ flew across the sky.

11. **kedss**   We sit at the _____ in our classroom.

men	eggs	vans	hands	jets	desks
dresses	ships	cats	jobs	bells	backs

Proofreading

Proofread the letter below. Use proofreading marks to correct four spelling mistakes, one capitalization mistake, and one punctuation mistake.

Proofreading Marks

◯ spell correctly
≡ capitalize
⊙ add period

James,

I went to the circus on its last day here. I watched the workers do their jobz. I saw mens put big cats in cages Some workers carried boxes on their backes, to put in vanz. they're going to your town next!

Sam

Entry Words

A singular word names one thing. To find a plural word in a dictionary, look for its singular form. For example, to find **cats**, look for **cat**.

> **cat** *plural* **cats.** A small furry animal. *Why is a **cat** a good pet? (Because it is purr-fect!)*

Write these plural words in alphabetical order. Then look each one up in a dictionary. Write the entry word and its page number.

Plural	Entry Word	Page
1. _____	_____	_____
2. _____	_____	_____
3. _____	_____	_____

unit 2 Review
Lessons 6-10

Lesson **6**

six

this

will

pick

Words with Short i

Write the spelling word for each meaning.

1. to choose something _____

2. the number before seven _____

3. going to _____

4. the thing here _____

Lesson **7**

live

give

think

sister

More Words with Short i

Write the spelling word for each clue.

5. what you do with a present _____

6. what a girl can be _____

7. what you do with your brain _____

8. what you do in your home _____

not

block

was

what

Words with Short o

Write the spelling word that completes each sentence.

9. I put a red _____ on top of the blue one.

10. Mr. Silva _____ not at school yesterday.

11. Tell me _____ you want to eat.

12. Leo is going, but I am _____.

LESSON 9

stop

clock

want

wash

More Words with Short o

Unscramble the letters in dark type to make a spelling word. Write the word to complete the sentence.

13. **natw** I _____ to go home now.

14. **locck** The _____ has stopped ticking.

15. **stpo** Please _____ the car at the corner.

16. **shwa** I have to _____ this messy shirt.

LESSON 10

hands

desks

dresses

men

Plural Words

Write the spelling word that belongs in each group.

17. ears, _____, feet

18. tables, chairs, _____

19. women, _____, children

20. _____, coats, hats

Words with Short u

sun	club	bug	mud	bus	up	of
under	run	from	summer	us	cut	but

bus

Say and Listen

Say each spelling word. Listen for the vowel sound you hear in sun.

Think and Sort

The vowel sound in sun is called short u. All of the spelling words have the short u sound. Spell each word aloud.

Look at the letters in each word. Think about how short u is spelled. How many spellings for short u do you see?

1. Write the **twelve** spelling words that have short u spelled u, like sun.

2. Write the **two** spelling words that have short u spelled o, like from.

1. u Words

_____   _____

_____   _____

_____   _____

_____   _____

_____   _____

_____   _____

2. o Words

_____   _____

Antonyms

Antonyms are words that have opposite meanings. Write the spelling word that is an antonym of each underlined word.

1. climb <u>down</u> the pole   _____

2. <u>over</u> the trees   _____

3. a letter <u>to</u> you   _____

4. gave <u>them</u> a gift   _____

5. <u>winter</u> days   _____

6. everyone <u>including</u> me   _____

7. <u>walk</u> to the store   _____

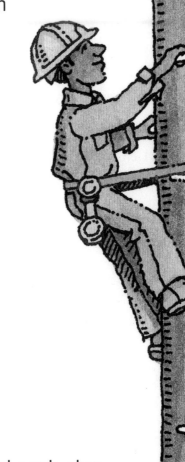

Hink Pinks

Hink pinks are funny pairs of rhyming words. Read each clue. Write the spelling word that completes each hink pink.

8. a big thing that Gus drives   Gus _____

9. what you can have on a sunny day   _____ fun

10. a place to get your hair trimmed   _____ hut

11. what a baby bear uses for golf   cub _____

12. a mat made for ants and beetles   _____ rug

13. a baby rose made of dirt and water   _____ bud

sun	club	bug	mud	bus	up	of
under	run	from	summer	us	cut	but

Proofreading

Proofread the ad below. Use proofreading marks to correct four spelling mistakes, one capitalization mistake, and one punctuation mistake.

Proofreading Marks

◯ spell correctly
≡ capitalize
⊙ add period

Come to Camp Beans!

You can hike upp a hill and catch a buge. you can sit in the sunn or read undr a tree You can even swim and fish in Beans Lake. Join us for the summer!

Call (101) 001-1010

Action Words

Some words in a sentence tell what someone does or did.
These words are called action words.

> hop   skips   talked   ran

Complete each sentence with an action word from one of the boxes.

cut   jump   shut   run   dug

1. I _____ races with my brother.

2. My mother _____ my hair.

3. How high can you _____?

4. Please _____ the door.

5. The mole _____ a hole.

More Words with Short u

just	jump	come	skunk	truck	lunch	other
brother	such	love	much	mother	one	fun

Say and Listen

Say each spelling word. Listen for the short u sound.

skunk

Think and Sort

All of the spelling words have the short u sound. Spell each word aloud.

Look at the letters in each word. Think about how short u is spelled.

1. Write the **eight** spelling words that have short u spelled u, like just.

2. Write the **six** spelling words that have short u spelled o, like come. Circle the three words that have a silent e at the end.

1. u Words

_____   _____

_____   _____

_____   _____

_____   _____

2. o Words

_____   _____

_____   _____

_____   _____

Word Meanings

Write the spelling word for each meaning.
Use a dictionary if you need to.

1. a good time   _____

2. a lot   _____

3. exactly   _____

4. very   _____

5. to like a lot   _____

6. different   _____

Partner Words

Complete each sentence. Write the spelling word that goes
with the underlined word.

7. The cats <u>go</u> out in the morning and _____ in at night.

8. A rabbit can <u>hop</u>. A frog can _____.

9. The girl is a <u>sister</u>. The boy is a _____.

10. A <u>father</u> is a man. A _____ is a woman.

11. We eat _____ at noon and <u>dinner</u> at six.

12. I have _____ nose and <u>two</u> eyes.

13. Will we ride in a _____ or fly in a <u>plane</u>?

just	jump	come	skunk	truck	lunch	other
brother	such	love	much	mother	one	fun

Proofreading

Proofread the letter below. Use proofreading marks to correct four spelling mistakes, one capitalization mistake, and one punctuation mistake

Proofreading Marks

◯ spell correctly

≡ capitalize

? add question mark

Ben,

We got a skunk! My muther and i put

him in our garage. He is fun to watch.

Mom jist came home in the truk. It is

time for lonch. Will you come over and

see our skunk this afternoon

Theo

Exclamation Points

Use an exclamation point at the end
of a sentence that shows strong
feeling or surprise.

> My frog won a blue ribbon!

The words in each sentence below are out of order.
Put the words in order and write the sentence correctly.
Remember to put an exclamation point at the end.

1. are fun Frog contests

_____

2. at has my brother frog Look the

_____

3. can jump high very That frog

_____

4. feet It jump more can ten than

_____

Words with Long a

game	today	play	whale	name	brave	maybe
baby	came	bake	ate	say	stay	gave

Say and Listen

Say each spelling word. Listen for the vowel sound you hear in game.

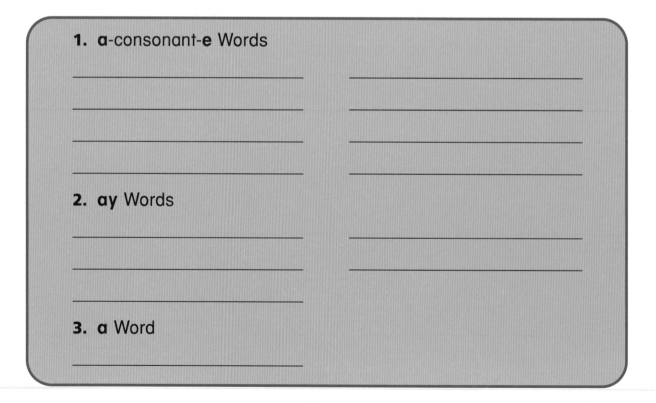

whales

Think and Sort

The vowel sound in game is called long a.
All of the spelling words have the long a sound. Spell each word aloud.

Look at the letters in each word. Think about how long a is spelled.

1. Write the **eight** words with long a spelled a-consonant-e, like game.

2. Write the **five** words with long a spelled ay, like stay.

3. Write the **one** word with long a spelled a.

1. a-consonant-e Words

_____   _____

_____   _____

_____   _____

_____

2. ay Words

_____   _____

_____   _____

_____

3. a Word

_____

Synonyms

Synonyms are words that have the same meaning.
Write the spelling word that is a synonym for each word below.

1. cook _____

2. fearless _____

3. speak _____

4. perhaps _____

5. wait _____

Word Meanings

Write the spelling word for each meaning.
Use a dictionary if you need to.

6. to have fun _____

7. this day _____

8. contest played with rules _____

9. handed over _____

10. what a person or thing is called _____

11. swallowed food _____

12. a young child _____

13. moved towards _____

| game | today | play | whale | name | brave | maybe |
| baby | came | bake | ate | say | stay | gave |

Proofreading

Proofread the diary page below. Use proofreading marks to correct four spelling mistakes, one capitalization mistake, and one punctuation mistake.

Proofreading Marks

◯ spell correctly
≡ capitalize
⊙ add period

December 12

Dear Diary,

   Alex tate cam to my home. We ate snacks. Then we talked about the gaem. Alex said that the best pley was at the end Then he gave me a football with his name on it. I can't wait to show it to Jake. Todae was a great day!

ABC Order

The words in a dictionary are in ABC order. Many words begin with the same letter, so the second letter is used to put them in ABC order.

Look at the two words below. Both words begin with **b**. The second letter must be used to put the words in ABC order. The letter **a** comes before **r**, so **bag** comes before **break**.

bag   break

Write the following words in alphabetical order.

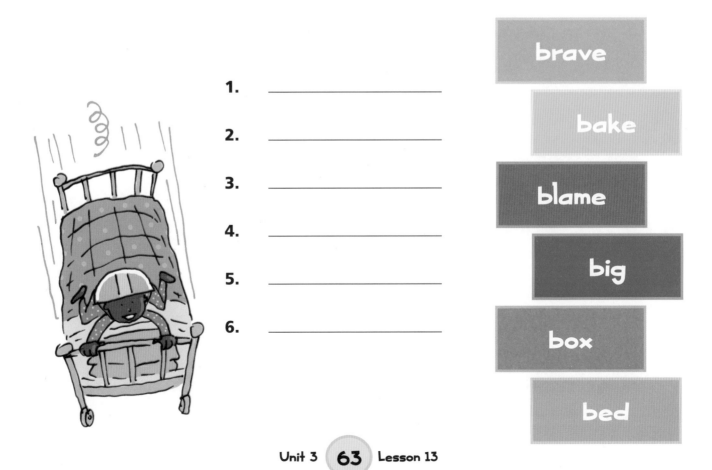

1. _____

2. _____

3. _____

4. _____

5. _____

6. _____

brave

bake

blame

big

box

bed

More Words with Long a

| chain | eight | paint | pail | snail | wait | train |
| gain | tail | nail | they | rain | mail | sail |

Say and Listen

Say each spelling word. Listen for the long a sound.

train

Think and Sort

All of the spelling words have the long a sound. Spell each word aloud.

Look at the letters in each word. Think about how long a is spelled. How many spellings for long a do you see?

1. Write the **twelve** spelling words that have long a spelled ai, like pail.

2. Write the **one** spelling word that has long a spelled ei.

3. Write the **one** spelling word that has long a spelled ey.

1. ai Words

_____   _____
_____   _____
_____   _____
_____   _____
_____   _____
_____   _____

2. ei Word   **3. ey** Word

_____   _____

Word Groups

Write the spelling word that belongs in each group.

1. wind, snow, _____

2. boat, plane, _____

3. hammer, saw, _____

4. grow, add, _____

5. draw, color, _____

6. turtle, worm, _____

7. he, she, _____

8. leash, rope, _____

Homophones

Homophones are words that sound the same but have different spellings and meanings. Complete each sentence by writing the spelling word that is a homophone for the underlined word.

9. The _____ for your boat is on <u>sale</u>.

10. He turned <u>pale</u> when he dropped the _____.

11. Jesse <u>ate</u> breakfast at _____.

12. I had to _____ for him to lift the <u>weight</u>.

13. The <u>tale</u> was about a cat with a long _____.

chain	eight	paint	pail	snail	wait	train
gain	tail	nail	they	rain	mail	sail

Proofreading

Proofread the letter below. Use proofreading marks to correct four spelling mistakes, one capitalization mistake, and one punctuation mistake.

Proofreading Marks

◯ spell correctly

≡ capitalize

? add question mark

625 Oak Street

Columbus, OH 43216

June 10, 2004

Dear Andrew,

   I can't waite until you come to see me! are you going to take the trane I am getting a pet snale in eighte days. I will let you hold it.

Your friend,

Malik

More Than One Meaning

Some words have more than one meaning. Read the entry for **paint** in a dictionary. **Paint** has two meanings. Each meaning has a number in front of it.

> **paint 1.** *plural* **paints.** Something to color with. *We bought blue paint for the walls in my room.* **2.** To cover something with paint. *Please don't paint our front porch and steps purple!* **painted, painting**

Write **1** or **2** to tell which meaning of **paint** is used in each sentence.

1. My father will paint my room yellow. _____

2. We bought the paint for my room yesterday. _____

3. I spilled paint on the rug. _____

4. Will you help me paint the fence? _____

5. Do you want to draw or paint? _____

Words with ed or ing

helping   wishing   fishing   picking   handed   thinking   fished
tricked   ended   wished   dressing   thanked   asked   catching

Say and Listen

Say the spelling words.
Listen for the ending sounds.

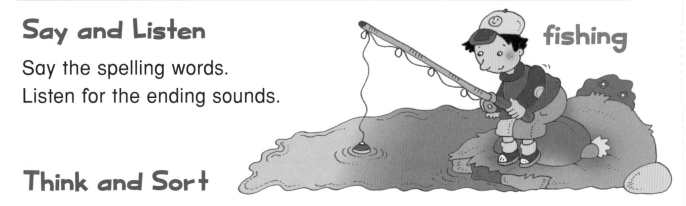

fishing

Think and Sort

A **base word** is a word that can be used to make other words.

Each spelling word is made of a base word and the ending ed or ing.

Look at each word. Think about the base word and the ending.
Spell each word aloud.

1. Write the **seven** spelling words that end in ed, like fished.

2. Write the **seven** spelling words that end in ing, like fishing.

1. ed Words

_____   _____
_____   _____
_____   _____
_____

2. ing Words

_____   _____
_____   _____
_____   _____
_____

Antonyms

Antonyms are words that have opposite meanings. Write the spelling word that is an antonym of each word below.

1. answered   _____

2. began   _____

3. hurting   _____

4. throwing   _____

Clues

Write the spelling word for each clue.

5. what you did if you caught some fish   _____

6. what you did if you were polite   _____

7. what you did when you hoped   _____

8. sitting with bait at the end of a pole   _____

9. taking an apple from a tree   _____

10. putting clothes on   _____

11. what someone did to play a joke on you   _____

12. what you are doing if you are hoping   _____

13. using your brain   _____

helping   wishing   fishing   picking   handed   thinking   fished

tricked   ended   wished   dressing   thanked   asked   catching

Proofreading

Proofread the paragraph below. Use proofreading marks to correct four spelling mistakes, one capitalization mistake, and one punctuation mistake.

Proofreading Marks

◯ spell correctly
= capitalize
⊙ add period

The race ended, and Turtle won.

He thankd Owl for the ribbon Rabbit felt

triked. he wishd that he had won. Rabbit

was not very smart. He should not have

gone fisheng.

Present and Past Tenses

Words that end with ed tell about the past. Words that end with ing tell about now or something that keeps going on. Write the word from the gift box that completes each sentence.

1. I _____ Pam rake leaves when it started to rain.

2. I like _____ Pam, but not in the rain!

3. Yesterday I _____ for directions to Jim's party.

4. I got lost on the way, so I kept _____ for directions.

5. My brother _____ me into doing his chores.

6. Everyone was _____ me on April Fool's Day.

unit 3 Review
LeSSons 11–15

Lesson **11**

cut
under
from
of

Words with Short u

Write the spelling word that completes each sentence and rhymes with the underlined word.

1. The <u>thunder</u> sent little Jim _____ the bed.

2. Victoria and I <u>love</u> the color _____ the sky.

3. It is hard to _____ a <u>nut</u>.

4. The <u>hum</u> came _____ my room.

Lesson **12**

much
just
other
come

More Words with Short u

Unscramble the letters in dark type to make a spelling word. Write the word to complete the sentence.

5. **emoc** Will Grandmother _____ to the party?

6. **sjut** This book is _____ what I wanted.

7. **umhc** We ate too _____ popcorn at the movie.

8. **tehor** Mom liked the _____ shirt more than this one.

Lesson **13**

gave

maybe

say

baby

Words with Long a

Write the spelling word that goes with the underlined word or words.

9. A <u>mother</u> is big. A _____ is small.

10. We <u>sing</u> songs. We _____ words.

11. Tim <u>handed</u> me a frog. I _____ it right back.

12. Mom and Dad didn't say <u>yes</u> or <u>no</u>. They said

_____.

Lesson **14**

train

wait

eight

they

More Words with Long a

Write the spelling word that completes each sentence.

13. My dog had _____ puppies.

14. The _____ was an hour late.

15. I will _____ for you after school.

16. Are _____ your brothers?

Lesson **15**

asked

thanked

helping

thinking

Words with ed or ing

Write the spelling word for each meaning.

17. using the mind _____

18. questioned someone _____

19. said that you were grateful _____

20. doing something useful _____

Words with Long e

we	people	she	keep	these	street	being
see	green	he	feet	bees	week	three

Say and Listen

Say each spelling word. Listen for the vowel sound you hear in we.

bee

Think and Sort

The vowel sound in we is called long e. All of the spelling words have the long e sound. Spell each word aloud.

1. Write the **four** words with long e spelled e, like we.

2. Write the **eight** words with long e spelled ee, like keep.

3. Write the **one** word with long e spelled e-consonant-e.

4. Write the **one** word with long e spelled eo.

1. e Words

_____ _____

_____ _____

2. ee Words

_____ _____

_____ _____

_____ _____

_____ _____

3. e-consonant-e Word   **4. eo Word**

_____ _____

Word Groups

Write the spelling word that belongs in each group.

1. ants, wasps, _____

2. yellow, _____, red

3. legs, _____, toes

4. _____, him, his

5. day, _____, month

6. _____, her, hers

7. them, those, _____

8. _____, us, our

Synonyms

Synonyms are words that have the same meaning. Write the spelling word that is a synonym for each word below.

9. look _____

10. persons _____

11. road _____

12. acting _____

13. save _____

we	people	she	keep	these	street	being
see	green	he	feet	bees	week	three

Proofreading

Proofread the newspaper story below. Use proofreading marks to correct four spelling mistakes, one capitalization mistake, and one punctuation mistake.

Proofreading Marks

◯ spell correctly
≡ capitalize
⊙ add period

Sports Buzz

Redtown Runners Take a Swim

Early Friday morning the peopel of Redtown stood along the streete by the park. They waited for the runners to pass by them. soon they saw the runners jumping around and waving their hands. Some beez were chasing them! The runners jumped in the pond to kep from being stung The race was over!

Language Connection

Capital Letters

Use a capital letter to begin the names of cities and states.

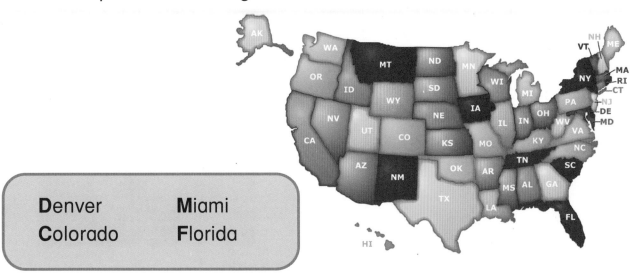

Denver   **M**iami
Colorado   **F**lorida

The sentences below have mistakes in capital letters and spelling. Write each sentence correctly.

1. I have been to ohio threa times.

_____

2. My grandfather is in dallas this weke.

_____

3. Theez trees grow all over maine.

_____

4. We went to se my aunt in seattle.

_____

More Words with Long e

| happy | very | leap | peach | city | puppy | penny |
| clean | please | funny | eat | heat | dream | mean |

Say and Listen

Say each spelling word. Listen for the long e sound.

Think and Sort

All of the spelling words have the long e sound.
Spell each word aloud.

Look at the letters in each word. Think about how long e is spelled.
How many spellings for long e do you see?

1. Write the **eight** spelling words that have long e spelled ea, like eat.

2. Write the **six** spelling words that have long e spelled y, like happy.

1. ea Words

_____   _____

_____   _____

_____   _____

_____   _____

2. y Words

_____   _____

_____   _____

_____   _____

Antonyms

Antonyms are words that have opposite meanings. Write the spelling word that is an antonym of the word in dark type.

1. The clown made us feel _____. **sad**

2. Please wear a _____ shirt. **dirty**

3. Do not be _____ to animals. **kind**

4. You can _____ this in the oven. **cool**

Clues

Write the spelling word for each clue.

5. This place has many people and buildings. _____

6. Say this to ask for something. _____

7. This fruit has a fuzzy skin. _____

8. Frogs do this to move. _____

9. Use this word instead of **silly**. _____

10. People do this to food. _____

11. Every big dog was once this. _____

12. This coin is worth one cent. _____

13. When you are asleep, you do this. _____

happy	very	leap	peach	city	puppy	penny
clean	please	funny	eat	heat	dream	mean

Proofreading

Proofread the letter below. Use proofreading marks to correct four spelling mistakes, one capitalization mistake, and one punctuation mistake.

Proofreading Marks

◯ spell correctly

= capitalize

⊙ add period

233 Park Lane

peru, IL 61354

April 12, 2004

Dear John,

I found a verry old peny last week I made it

bright and cleen. I am going to take it to a coin

show in the citty. Will you go with me?

Your friend,

Anton

Dictionary Skills

Guide Words

Every dictionary page has two guide words at the top. The first guide word is the first entry word on the page. The second guide word is the last entry word on the page.

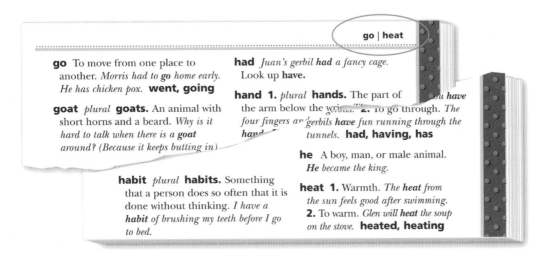

Write these entry words in alphabetical order. Then look up each one in a dictionary. Write the guide words for the page.

happy   **eat**   **leap**

Entry Word   Guide Words

1. _____   _____ _____

2. _____   _____ _____

3. _____   _____ _____

Words with Long i

like	ice	side	write	ride	eye	inside
find	bike	nine	mine	white	hide	five

Say and Listen

Say each spelling word. Listen for the vowel sound you hear in like.

bike

Think and Sort

The vowel sound in like is called long i. All of the spelling words have the long i sound. Spell each word aloud.

Look at the letters in each word. Think about how long i is spelled.

1. Write the **twelve** words with long i spelled i-consonant-e, like ride.

2. Write the **one** word with long i spelled i.

3. Write the **one** word with long i spelled eye.

---

1. i-consonant-e Words

_____ _____

_____ _____

_____ _____

_____ _____

_____ _____

_____ _____

2. i Word **3. eye Word**

_____ _____

Word Meanings

Write the spelling word for each meaning.
Use a dictionary if you need to.

1. something with wheels to ride on _____

2. to enjoy _____

3. to sit on and be carried _____

4. the lightest color _____

5. to make words with a pencil _____

6. into _____

Rhymes

Write the spelling word that completes each sentence
and rhymes with the underlined word.

7. Let's _____ out how to <u>wind</u> the clock.

8. Did you <u>try</u> to blink your left _____?

9. Did the cat _____ under the <u>slide</u>?

10. We planted all _____ of the <u>pine</u> trees.

11. The left _____ of the road is <u>wide</u>.

12. I slipped <u>twice</u> on the snow and _____.

13. Her soup is cold, but _____ is <u>fine</u>.

like	ice	side	write	ride	eye	inside
find	bike	nine	mine	white	hide	five

Proofreading

Proofread the letter below. Use proofreading marks to correct four spelling mistakes, one capitalization mistake, and one punctuation mistake.

Proofreading Marks

◯ spell correctly

≡ capitalize

⊙ add period

Hi, Allie!

    I really liek Alaska. Today we rode a

sled over the ise. a team of wite dogs

pulled us. We rode for five miles Then we

went insid our cabin and lit a fire. Write

and tell me how your new kitten is doing.

What's her name?

             Meg

Present and Past Tenses

Some words show action happening now, or in the present. Some words show action in the past. Look at the chart below. Notice the different spellings.

Present	Past
do	did
find	found
ride	rode

Choose the correct word in dark type to complete each sentence. Write the word on the line.

1. Watch my kittens (**hide**, **hid**) under my bed. _____

2. They (**hide**, **hid**) there last night, too. _____

3. Dad (**write**, **wrote**) a silly story for us. _____

4. We can (**write**, **wrote**) a poem about him. _____

5. Do you (**like**, **liked**) to ice skate? _____

6. Mom (**like**, **liked**) the present we gave her. _____

More Words with Long i

sky	tiny	lion	why	try	high	my
pie	cry	tie	by	tiger	lie	fly

Say and Listen

Say each spelling word. Listen for the long i sound.

tiger

Think and Sort

All of the spelling words have the long i sound. Spell each word aloud.

Look at the letters in each word. Think about how long i is spelled.

1. Write the **three** spelling words with long i spelled i, like tiny.

2. Write the **seven** spelling words with long i spelled y, like sky.

3. Write the **three** spelling words with long i spelled ie, like lie.

4. Write the **one** spelling word with long i spelled igh.

1. i Words _____

_____ _____

2. y Words _____

_____ _____

_____ _____

_____

3. ie Words _____

_____ _____

4. igh Word _____

Antonyms

Antonyms are words that have opposite meanings. Write the spelling word that is an antonym of each underlined word.

1. The cat climbed to the <u>low</u> branch. _____

2. Don't <u>laugh</u> over spilled milk. _____

3. Look at that <u>large</u> mouse! _____

4. He was sorry he told the <u>truth</u>. _____

5. This is <u>your</u> hat. _____

What's Missing?

Write the missing spelling words.

6. eat _____ and ice cream

7. wear a shirt and _____

8. the mane on the _____

9. _____ and try again

10. don't know _____

11. clouds in the _____

12. stripes on the _____

13. sit _____ him

sky	tiny	lion	why	try	high	my
pie	cry	tie	by	tiger	lie	fly

Proofreading

Proofread the journal page below. Use proofreading marks to correct four spelling mistakes, one capitalization mistake, and one punctuation mistake.

Proofreading Marks
⭕ spell correctly
= capitalize
⊙ add period

march 3

Today the skye was very blue. The clouds were

big and fluffy. I drew a tiger on some paper

and made a kite with it. I wanted the kite to

touch a cloud. It looked tinee in the air, but it

did not flie high enough I will trie again next

week. Maybe then my kite will touch a cloud.

More Than One Meaning

Some words have more than one meaning. Study the dictionary entry below for **tie**. Then write the number of the meaning that best fits each sentence below.

> **tie 1.** *plural* **ties.** A necktie.
> *He spilled something on his* **tie.**
> **2.** An equal score. *The banana-eating contest ended in a* **tie. 3.** To attach something with string or rope.
> *She tried to* **tie** *Mei's shoelaces together.*
> **tied, tying**

Meaning

1. Will you please **tie** my shoelaces for me? _____

2. The frog-jumping contest ended in a **tie**. _____

3. Dad should wear a **tie** to Robin's party. _____

4. **Tie** this rope around the tree trunk. _____

5. The man's **tie** matched his shirt. _____

More Words with ed or ing

dropping dropped stopping jogged running hopping dotted
cutting spotted hopped jogging shopped stopped shopping

Say and Listen

Say the spelling words.
Listen for the ending sounds.

running

Think and Sort

Each spelling word is made by adding ed or ing to a base word.
Each base word ends with a short vowel and consonant.

Look at the letters in each spelling word. Think about how the base
word changes when ed or ing is added. Spell each word aloud.

1. Write the **seven** spelling words that end in ed, like hopped.

2. Write the **seven** spelling words that end in ing, like hopping.

---

1. ed Words

_____   _____

_____   _____

_____   _____

_____

2. ing Words

_____   _____

_____   _____

_____   _____

_____

Word Meanings

Write the spelling word for each meaning.

1. moved up and down quickly   _____

2. moving at a slow, steady trot   _____

3. marked with a round point   _____

4. ended   _____

5. looked for things to buy   _____

6. let something fall   _____

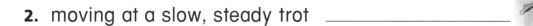

Synonyms

Synonyms are words that have the same meaning. Write the spelling word that is a synonym for each word in dark type.

7. The apples are _____ off the tree. **falling**

8. The woman _____ around the block. **trotted**

9. We saw that the rain was _____. **ending**

10. The children are _____ on one foot. **jumping**

11. We saw a man _____ to his car. **racing**

12. The spilled paint _____ the floor. **marked**

13. Mom is _____ for some new shoes. **looking**

dropping	dropped	stopping	jogged	running	hopping	dotted
cutting	spotted	hopped	jogging	shopped	stopped	shopping

Proofreading

Proofread the postcard below. Use proofreading marks to correct four spelling mistakes, one capitalization mistake, and one punctuation mistake.

Proofreading Marks

◯ spell correctly

≡ capitalize

? add question mark

Dear Juan,

I went joging today along the beach. I jogd for a long time. there was no stopin me. Everyone stopped to wave at me as I went runnig by. What are you doing for fun

Your friend,

Hector

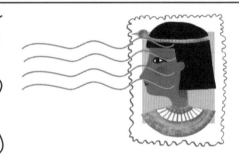

Juan Bravo

7601 Water Road

Houston, TX 77035

Verb Forms

Some words show action. These words are called verbs, and they have different forms. Look at the box below. Notice the different forms of the verb.

> Dad likes to **jog** every day.
> Mom **jogged** with him last week.
> Scooter is **jogging** with him today.

Choose the correct verb in dark type to complete each sentence. Write the word on the line.

1. Maria will be (**shop**, **shopping**) in town. _____

2. I (**shop**, **shopped**) for shoes last week. _____

3. Nathan was (**hop**, **hopping**) like a rabbit. _____

4. His pet frog (**hop**, **hopped**) right out of its bowl! _____

5. Dad (**stop**, **stopped**) the car at the light. _____

6. The bus is (**stop**, **stopping**) at every corner. _____

unit 4 Review
lessons 16-20

Lesson **16**

being
street
week
people

Words with Long e

Write the spelling word that completes each sentence.

1. I like _____ with my grandfather.
2. Our vacation starts in a _____.
3. A lot of cars were on the _____.
4. My dad invited fifty _____ to his party.

Lesson **17**

clean
please
very
funny

More Words with Long e

Write the spelling word for each meaning.

5. not dirty   _____
6. really   _____
7. silly   _____
8. be so kind as to   _____

Lesson **18**

write
white
find
eye

Words with Long i

Write the spelling word that belongs in each group.

9. read, _____, count
10. ear, nose, _____
11. see, look, _____
12. black, _____, gray

tiny

why

tie

high

More Words with Long i

Write the spelling word for each clue.

13. A man wears this around his neck.

_____

14. This word means "very small."

_____

15. Use this word to ask for a reason.

_____

16. This word is the opposite of **low**.

_____

dropped

stopped

running

hopping

More Words with ed or ing

Write the spelling word that completes each sentence.

17. The rabbit was _____ across our lawn.

18. The rain _____ in time for our picnic.

19. I _____ all the dishes on the floor!

20. Ling is _____ to catch up with us.

Words with Long o

go	home	grow	no	hope	snow	hole
yellow	rope	know	nose	stone	so	joke

Say and Listen

Say each spelling word. Listen for the
vowel sound you hear in go.

Think and Sort

yellow

The vowel sound in all of the spelling words is called long o.
Spell each word aloud.

Look at the letters in each word. Think about how long o is spelled.

1. Write the **three** spelling words with long o spelled o, like go.

2. Write the **seven** spelling words with long o spelled o-consonant-e,
   like hole.

3. Write the **four** spelling words with long o spelled ow, like snow.

1. o Words

_____   _____

_____

2. o-consonant-e Words

_____   _____

_____   _____

_____   _____

_____

3. ow Words

_____   _____

_____   _____

Word Groups

Write the spelling word that belongs in each group.

1. rain, _____, ice

2. red, blue, _____

3. eye, ear, _____

4. yes, _____, maybe

5. string, yarn, _____

Rhymes

Write the spelling word that completes
each sentence and rhymes with the underlined word.

6. I left my brush and <u>comb</u> at _____.

7. The tiny <u>mole</u> ran down a _____.

8. I _____ you like the fancy <u>soap</u>.

9. The dinosaur <u>bone</u> turned to _____.

10. Ned <u>woke</u> me up to tell me a _____.

11. Corn plants will _____ in each <u>row</u>.

12. The <u>bow</u> was _____ big that it hid the package.

13. I cannot _____ skating with a sore <u>toe</u>.

go	home	grow	no	hope	snow	hole
yellow	rope	know	nose	stone	so	joke

Proofreading

Proofread the letter below. Use proofreading marks to correct four spelling mistakes, one capitalization mistake, and one punctuation mistake.

Proofreading Marks

◯ spell correctly

≡ capitalize

? add question mark

1212 Rose Avenue

Rock Springs, WY 82942

January 19, 2003

Dear Ling,

Can you goe on a ski trip We can have fun.

The trails are marked with yellow rop. I hope

the snowe is deep. last year I hit a ston and

broke my ski.

Your friend,

Luisa

Homophones

Some words sound the same but have different spellings and different meanings. These words are called homophones. **Our** and **hour** are homophones.

Choose the correct homophone in dark type to complete each sentence. Write the word on the line.

1. "I ate the (**hole**, **whole**) doughnut," said Max. _____

2. "Did you eat the (**hole**, **whole**) in the middle, too?" asked Mia.

   _____

3. Did you (**no**, **know**) that our sun is really a star? _____

4. There is (**no**, **know**) way to count all the stars. _____

5. "I will (**sew**, **so**) a new dress for Meg," said my mom.

   _____

6. "And (**so**, **sew**) will I," said Aunt Jane. _____

7. "She will look (**so**, **sew**) pretty," said my mom. _____

More Words with Long o

cold	gold	old	sold	open	roll	hold
road	goat	coat	boat	over	most	told

Say and Listen

Say each spelling word. Listen for the long o sound.

goat

Think and Sort

All of the spelling words have the long o sound. Spell each word aloud.

Look at the letters in each word. Think about how long o is spelled. How many spellings for long o do you see?

1. Write the **ten** spelling words that have long o spelled o, like cold.

2. Write the **four** spelling words that have long o spelled oa, like goat.

1. o Words

_____   _____

_____   _____

_____   _____

_____   _____

_____   _____

2. oa Words

_____   _____

_____   _____

Letter Scramble

Unscramble the letters in dark type to make a spelling word.
Write the word on the line.

1. **dols** bought and _____

2. **roev** under or _____

3. **atoc** _____ and hat

4. **locd** hot and _____

5. **enpo** _____ or closed

Clues

Write the spelling word for each clue.

6. This travels on the water. _____

7. This word means "did tell." _____

8. Many rings are made of this. _____

9. A car drives on this. _____

10. This farm animal has horns. _____

11. You can do this to someone's hand. _____

12. The opposite of **new** is this. _____

13. This word rhymes with **toast**. _____

cold	gold	old	sold	open	roll	hold
road	goat	coat	boat	over	most	told

Proofreading

Proofread the ad below. Use proofreading marks to correct four spelling mistakes, one capitalization mistake, and one punctuation mistake.

Proofreading Marks
- ◯ spell correctly
- ≡ capitalize
- ⊙ add period

Goat Boat Rides!

Take a ride on a snow boat! It is the moast fun you will ever have! our brown and goeld goats will pull you in a boat. You will fly across the snow We are open six days a week. Wear a heavy cote so that you will not get coald.

Synonyms and Antonyms

Synonyms are words that have the same meaning. Antonyms are words that have opposite meanings.

Synonyms	Antonyms
little, small	tall, short

Use a word from the boxes to write a synonym for each word.

 road    gold    told   roll

1. street _____   **2.** said _____

3. bun _____   **4.** yellow _____

Use a word from the boxes to write an antonym for each word.

 cold    open    over    old

5. under _____   **6.** shut _____

7. new _____   **8.** hot _____

The Vowel Sound in book

| book | look | pull | cook | full | cookies | foot |
| put | could | would | should | stood | good | took |

Say and Listen

Say each spelling word. Listen for the vowel sound you hear in book.

book

Think and Sort

All of the spelling words have the vowel sound in book. Spell each word aloud.

Look at the letters in each word. Think about how the vowel sound in book is spelled.

1. Write the **eight** spelling words that have oo, like book.

2. Write the **three** spelling words that have ou, like could.

3. Write the **three** spelling words that have u, like put.

1. oo Words

_____   _____

_____   _____

_____   _____

_____   _____

2. ou Words

_____   _____

_____   _____

3. u Words

_____   _____

_____

Word Meanings

Write the spelling word for each meaning.

1. small, sweet cakes   _____

2. a form of the word **will**   _____

3. someone who makes food   _____

4. to set something in place   _____

5. pages fastened together   _____

6. was able to do something   _____

7. was upright on the feet   _____

8. to have a duty   _____

9. see   _____

Antonyms

Antonyms are words that have opposite meanings. Complete each sentence by writing the spelling word that is an antonym of the word in dark type.

10. Rita will _____ your sled up the hill.   **push**

11. Mason _____ a cookie to school.   **gave**

12. The cookie jar was _____.   **empty**

13. This spaghetti tastes _____.   **bad**

book	look	pull	cook	full	cookies	foot
put	could	would	should	stood	good	took

Proofreading

Proofread the ad below. Use proofreading marks to correct four spelling mistakes, one capitalization mistake, and one punctuation mistake.

Proofreading Marks

◯ spell correctly
= capitalize
⊙ add period

Woud you like a treat? Come to the

Milk and Cookies Shop at 16 oak Street.

Our shop is ful of delicious

cookies Take a good looke.

Try some. Buy some.

Our cok is the best!

Language Connection

Abbreviations

An abbreviation is a short way of writing a word. Abbreviations usually begin with a capital letter and end with a period.

Mister = **Mr.**	Mistress = **Mrs.**
Street = **St.**	Road = **Rd.**

The following names and addresses have mistakes.
Write each one correctly.

1. mr Roy Gray _____

2. 1631 Elm rd _____

3. mrs Jean Ryan _____

4. 402 Bank st. _____

5. mr. Yoshi Ono _____

6. 6800 Burnet rd. _____

7. mrs Deana Reyna _____

8. 509 State St _____

9. Mr Jackson Palmer _____

The Vowel Sound in zoo

zoo	to	new	food	blue	tooth	moon
too	do	room	who	school	soon	two

Say and Listen

Say each spelling word. Listen for the vowel sound you hear in zoo.

Think and Sort

All of the spelling words have the vowel sound in zoo. Spell each word aloud.

Look at the letters in each spelling word. Think about how the vowel sound in zoo is spelled.

1. Write the **eight** words with oo, like zoo.

2. Write the **one** word with ue.

3. Write the **one** word with ew.

4. Write the **four** words with o, like do.

1. oo Words

_____   _____

_____   _____

_____   _____

_____   _____

2. ue Word   **3. ew** Word

_____   _____

4. o Words

_____   _____

_____   _____

Word Meanings

Write the spelling word for each meaning.

1. a body that moves around a planet _____

2. which person _____

3. a place where wild animals are kept _____

4. something to eat _____

5. in a short time _____

6. a hard, bony growth in the mouth _____

7. a space in a building _____

Homophones

Homophones are words that sound the same but have different spellings and meanings. Write the spelling word that completes each sentence and is a homophone of the underlined word.

8. Our _____ umbrella <u>blew</u> away.

9. The <u>two</u> boys swam _____ the shore.

10. I <u>knew</u> that Nina had a _____ puppy.

11. How many books _____ we have <u>due</u> at the library?

12. They have _____ many things <u>to</u> do.

13. Did Chad score _____ points, <u>too</u>?

zoo	to	new	food	blue	tooth	moon
too	do	room	who	school	soon	two

Proofreading

Proofread the paragraph below.
Use proofreading marks to correct
four spelling mistakes, one
capitalization mistake, and
one punctuation mistake.

Proofreading Marks

◯ spell correctly

≡ capitalize

⊙ add period

> The Strange Fish
>
> Last summer I went fishing with my dad. I
> caught the strangest fish I had ever seen. dad
> thought it was tew strange to eat. I didn't
> know what to doo with it. Grandpa knew the
> place to call. He called the zue We soun found
> out that my fish was a mudfish.

Language Connection

Nouns

A noun is a word that names a person, place, or thing.

Person	Place	Thing
boy	city	toy
girl	town	dog

Find the noun in the box that completes each sentence.
Then write the sentence.

 room    zoo    tooth   moon

1. We saw lions and tigers at the ___.

_____

2. Chad lost a ___ at school.

_____

3. Which ___ should we paint next?

_____

4. The full ___ made the sky bright.

_____

More Words with ed or ing

| joking | baking | hoped | liked | lived | riding | loved |
| named | biked | living | giving | baked | writing | having |

Say and Listen

Say the spelling words.
Listen for the ending sounds.

baking

Think and Sort

Each spelling word is made by adding ed or ing to a base word. Each base word ends with e.

Look at the letters in each word. Think how the base word changes when ed or ing is added. Spell each word aloud.

1. Write the **seven** spelling words that end in ed, like liked.

2. Write the **seven** spelling words that end in ing, like joking.

1. ed Words

_____   _____

_____   _____

_____   _____

_____

2. ing Words

_____   _____

_____   _____

_____   _____

_____

Word Groups

Write the spelling word that belongs in each group.

1. hiked, skated, _____

2. reading, spelling, _____

3. frying, broiling, _____

4. laughing, teasing, _____

5. wanted, wished, _____

6. liked, cared, _____

Synonyms

Synonyms are words that have the same meaning. Complete each sentence by writing the spelling word that is a synonym for each word in dark type.

7. We _____ the dog Nicki.   **called**

8. We _____ a dozen cookies.   **cooked**

9. Mr. Reyna _____ in a house nearby.   **stayed**

10. We are _____ food to the birds.   **offering**

11. Are you _____ ice cream with your cake?   **getting**

12. I like _____ in the city.   **being**

13. Rosa will be _____ on a train.   **sitting**

| joking | baking | hoped | liked | lived | riding | loved |
| named | biked | living | giving | baked | writing | having |

Proofreading

Proofread the letter below.
Use proofreading marks to correct
four spelling mistakes, one
capitalization mistake, and
one punctuation mistake.

Proofreading Marks

◯ spell correctly

≡ capitalize

? add question mark

Franco,

    Yesterday I met a man named mr. Banana.

He was a funny man. He said he bakked a

bicycle. He hopd I liked it. He wanted me

to go rideng on it. Do you think he was

just jokking Could a person really bake

a bicycle?

                Peter

Dictionary Skills

Base Words

To find an **ed** or **ing** word in a dictionary, look for the base word entry. The **ed** and **ing** forms of a word are given as part of the base word entry.

Below are eight **ing** words. Write the base word for each one. Then look up each base word in a dictionary and write the page number for it.

	Base Word	Dictionary Page
1. living	_____	_____
2. giving	_____	_____
3. having	_____	_____
4. writing	_____	_____
5. loving	_____	_____
6. biking	_____	_____
7. naming	_____	_____
8. liking	_____	_____

unit 5 review
LESSONS 21-25

LESSON 21

no

home

know

yellow

Words with Long o

Write the spelling word for each clue.

1. This means that you understand something.

   _____

2. A lemon is this color. _____

3. This is the opposite of **yes**. _____

4. The place where you live is

   called this. _____

LESSON 22

cold

open

over

coat

More Words with Long o

Write the spelling word that belongs in each group.

5. sweater, jacket, _____

6. unlock, uncover, _____

7. cool, chilly, _____

8. under, beside, _____

 **LESSON 23**

book
could
would
pull
put

The Vowel Sound in **book**

Write the spelling word that completes each sentence.

9. I enjoyed reading this _____.

10. Dan, _____ you like some soup?

11. Don't _____ the rope too hard.

12. You need to _____ your clothes away.

13. Jay, you _____ wash the dishes.

 **LESSON 24**

tooth
two
blue
new

The Vowel Sound in **zoo**

Write the missing spelling word.

14. my missing _____

15. the deep _____ sea

16. one or _____ apples

17. old and _____

 **LESSON 25**

liked
riding
writing

More Words with **ed** or **ing**

Write the spelling word for each meaning.

18. making words with a pencil _____

19. enjoyed _____

20. sitting in and being carried _____

The Vowel Sound in out

out	town	now	flower	owl	how	cow
found	sound	mouse	round	around	house	clown

Say and Listen

Say each spelling word. Listen for the vowel sound you hear in out.

cow

Think and Sort

All of the spelling words have the vowel sound in out. Spell each word aloud.

Look at the letters in each word. Think about how the vowel sound in out is spelled.

1. Write the **seven** spelling words that have ou, like out.

2. Write the **seven** spelling words that have ow, like cow.

1. ou Words

_____   _____

_____   _____

_____   _____

_____

2. ow Words

_____   _____

_____   _____

_____   _____

_____

Letter Scramble

Unscramble each group of letters to make a spelling word. Write the word on the line.

1. lerfow   _____

2. undor   _____

3. droanu   _____

4. tou   _____

5. nudof   _____

Clues

Write the spelling word for each clue.

6. You see this person at the circus. _____

7. This is another word for **noise**. _____

8. This has a roof and a door. _____

9. Use this word to ask a question. _____

10. This bird is often called wise. _____

11. This is a small city. _____

12. A cat likes to chase this animal. _____

13. This word is the opposite of **then**. _____

out	town	now	flower	owl	how	cow
found	sound	mouse	round	around	house	clown

Proofreading

Proofread the postcard below.
Use proofreading marks to correct four
spelling mistakes, one capitalization
mistake, and one punctuation mistake.

Proofreading Marks
◯ spell correctly
≡ capitalize
? add question mark

Dear Bailey,

   I am drawing pictures of my
toun. First I walked arownd to
get ideas. I saw a mouse by a
tree. then I fownd a big green
hows. Do you like to draw Draw
me a picture of your town.

                Eric

Bailey Oakes

986 Tell Ave.

Ventura, IA

50482

Language Connection

Was and Were

The words **was** and **were** tell about the past. **Was** tells about one person or thing. **Were** tells about two or more persons or things.

I **was**	Jed **was**	the cat **was**
we **were**	Jed and Ted **were**	the cats **were**

Choose the correct word in dark type to complete each sentence. Then find the spelling mistake. Write the sentence correctly.

1. The dog (**was**, **were**) afraid of the sownd.

   _____

2. The boys (**was**, **were**) glad to see the oul.

   _____

3. The child (**was**, **were**) picking a flouer.

   _____

4. How many stores (**was**, **were**) in that toun?

   _____

5. A mous (**was**, **were**) hiding in my shoe.

   _____

The Vowel Sound in saw

saw	talk	call	off	draw	lost	walk
song	dog	frog	ball	all	small	long

Say and Listen

Say each spelling word. Listen for the vowel sound you hear in saw.

Think and Sort

All of the spelling words have the vowel sound in saw. Spell each word aloud.

frogs

Look at the letters in each word.
Think about how the vowel sound in saw is spelled.

1. Write the **two** spelling words that have aw, like saw.

2. Write the **six** spelling words that have a, like ball.

3. Write the **six** spelling words that have o, like dog.

1. **aw** Words

_____ _____

2. **a** Words

_____ _____

_____ _____

_____ _____

3. **o** Words

_____ _____

_____ _____

Word Groups

Write the spelling word that belongs in each group.

1. pup, hound, _____

2. yell, shout, _____

3. tadpole, toad, _____

4. run, jog, _____

5. speak, say, _____

6. paint, sketch, _____

7. looked, watched, _____

8. music, tune, _____

Antonyms

Antonyms are words that have opposite meanings. Complete each sentence by writing the spelling word that is an antonym of the word in dark type.

9. The room was very _____. **large**

10. Have you _____ your red hat? **found**

11. Last year her hair was _____. **short**

12. Please turn _____ the light. **on**

13. We found _____ of the missing screws. **none**

| saw | talk | call | off | draw | lost | walk |
| song | dog | frog | ball | all | small | long |

Proofreading

Proofread the letter below. Use proofreading marks to correct four spelling mistakes, one capitalization mistake, and one punctuation mistake.

Proofreading Marks

◯ spell correctly
= capitalize
⊙ add period

Dear Amy,

I have a smal dog named Chip. he has longe black hair He always comes when I cal him. Chip loves to chase a baul. Sometimes he doesn't want to give it back to me! Would you like to come play catch with us?

Daniel

Dictionary Skills

Using the Spelling Table

A spelling table can help you find words in a dictionary. A spelling table shows the different spellings for sounds. Suppose you are not sure how to spell the long **e** sound in **freeze**. First, find **long e** in the spelling table. Then read the first spelling for the sound and look up **frez** in a dictionary. Look for each spelling in the dictionary until you find the correct one.

Sound	Example Words	Spellings
long e	he, eat, tree, very, people, belief	e ea ee y eo ie

Complete each picture name by writing the correct letter or letters. Use the Spelling Table on page 141 and a dictionary to decide on the correct letters.

1.  l_____bster

2.  athl_____

3.  cl_____ver

4.  r_____ng

5.  sp_____n

6. _____ite

The Vowel Sound in for

for	door	story	snore	horse	four	floor
corn	or	short	more	storm	orange	store

Say and Listen

storm

Say each spelling word. Listen for the vowel sound you hear in for.

Think and Sort

All of the spelling words have the vowel sound in for. Spell each word aloud.

Look at the letters in each word. Think about how the vowel sound in for is spelled.

1. Write the **eleven** spelling words that have o or o-consonant-e, like for and more.

2. Write the **two** spelling words that have oo, like door.

3. Write the **one** spelling word that has ou.

1. o or **o**-consonant-**e** Words

_____   _____

_____   _____

_____   _____

_____   _____

_____   _____

_____

2. oo Words

_____   _____

3. ou Word

_____

Word Meanings

Write the spelling word for each meaning. Use a dictionary if you need to.

1. a yellow grain _____

2. very bad weather _____

3. a place where goods are sold _____

4. not tall _____

5. the number after three _____

6. a large four-legged animal with hooves _____

Clues

Write the spelling word for each clue.

7. You want this if you want extra. _____

8. This word is used on a gift card. _____

9. This word can join two others. _____

10. You can drink this juice for breakfast. _____

11. Some people do this when they sleep. _____

12. You go in and out through this. _____

13. People walk on this. _____

for	door	story	snore	horse	four		floor
corn	or	short	more	storm	orange		store

Proofreading

Proofread the ad below. Use proofreading marks to correct four spelling mistakes, one capitalization mistake, and one punctuation mistake.

Proofreading Marks

◯ spell correctly

≡ capitalize

⊙ add period

Fur and Feathers Pet Store

Feeding birds in your back yard can be fun. Our stoore has everything you need. We have cracked corne, sunflower seeds, and fruit. we also have special feeding dishes. Cut up an orinqe and put it on a feeding dish In a shart time, you will have lots of feathered visitors!

End Marks

Put a period (.) at the end of a sentence that tells something. Put a question mark (?) at the end of a question. Put an exclamation point (!) at the end of a sentence that shows strong feeling or surprise.

It was a nice day. When did it get cold?
Now we have three feet of snow!

Choose the correctly spelled word in dark type to complete each sentence. Then write the sentence, adding the correct end mark.

1. Snow has fallen for (**fower**, **four**) days and nights

_____

2. Watch out for the snow above that (**door**, **dore**)

_____

3. Do you think we will get (**more**, **mor**) snow

_____

The Vowel Sound in jar

jar	party	arm	mark	star	dark	far
car	barn	father	farmer	are	farm	art

Say and Listen

Say each spelling word. Listen for the vowel sound you hear in jar.

jar

Think and Sort

All of the spelling words have the vowel sound in jar. The sound is spelled a in each word. Look at the letters in each word. Spell each word aloud.

1. Write the **one** spelling word that has a.

2. Write the **thirteen** spelling words that have ar, like jar.

1. a Word

_____

2. ar Words

_____   _____

_____   _____

_____   _____

_____   _____

_____

Word Groups

Write the spelling word that belongs in each group.

1. gardener, rancher, _____

2. music, reading, _____

3. hand, wrist, _____

4. glass, bottle, _____

5. is, am, _____

6. garden, ranch, _____

7. brother, mother, _____

8. black, unlit, _____

Rhymes

Write the spelling word that completes each sentence
and rhymes with the underlined word.

9. You traveled _____ in your <u>car</u>.

10. Did <u>Marty</u> go to the _____?

11. The <u>shark</u> had a _____ on its fin.

12. How <u>far</u> away is that _____?

13. The cat carried the <u>yarn</u> to the _____.

jar	party	arm	mark	star	dark	far
car	barn	father	farmer	are	farm	art

Proofreading

Proofread the book jacket below.
Use proofreading marks to correct
four spelling mistakes, one
capitalization mistake, and
one punctuation mistake.

Proofreading Marks

◯ spell correctly
≡ capitalize
? add question mark

every summer night the Clark children have a pardy when it gets daark. They chase fireflies around the barne. One night a firefly lands on a child's arem. The firefly blinks a message. What is it trying to say Read <u>The Firefly Farm</u> to find out.

Dictionary Skills

More Than One Meaning

Some words have more than one meaning. The dictionary entries for these words give the different meanings. Study the entries below.

> **star** *plural* **stars. 1.** The sun and other bright heavenly bodies. *The **star** we see best at night is the North Star.* **2.** A leading actor or actress, athlete, or musician. *My brother is a super drummer. I think he will be a rock **star**!*

> **mark** *plural* **marks. 1.** A spot on something. *A wet glass will leave a **mark** on a table.* **2.** A grade given in school. *I got good **marks** on my report card.*

Use the correct word above to complete each sentence.
Then write the number of the meaning used in the sentence.

1. Everyone cheered for the _____ of the show. _____

2. Dad couldn't get the _____ off the car. _____

3. One _____ shone brighter than the others. _____

4. Kim got a high _____ on her art project. _____

5. Our sun is really a _____. _____

6. The pen left a _____ on the table. _____

Words with er

colder	helper	braver	writer	longer	flatter	painter
bigger	shopper	runner	older	jumper	faster	baker

Say and Listen

Say each spelling word. Listen for the ending sounds.

painter

Think and Sort

Each spelling word is made by adding er to a base word. In which spelling words does the spelling of the base word change?

1. Write the **seven** spelling words with no change in the base word, like colder.

2. Write the **four** spelling words in which the final consonant of the base word is doubled, like flatter.

3. Write the **three** spelling words in which the final e of the base word is dropped, like braver.

1. No Change in Base Word

_____   _____

_____   _____

_____   _____

_____

2. Final Consonant Doubled

_____   _____

_____   _____

3. Final **e** Dropped

_____   _____

_____

Word Meanings

Write the spelling word for each meaning.

1. someone who shops _____

2. someone who helps _____

3. someone who writes stories _____

4. more able to face danger _____

5. someone who runs _____

6. more flat _____

7. someone who jumps _____

8. one who colors things _____

Antonyms

Antonyms are words that have opposite meanings. Complete each sentence by writing the spelling word that is an antonym of the word in dark type.

9. Kay is _____ than her sister. **younger**

10. The turtle was _____ than the rabbit. **slower**

11. My legs are _____ than yours. **shorter**

12. Jesse's feet are _____ than mine. **smaller**

13. The night was _____ than the day. **hotter**

colder	helper	braver	writer	longer	flatter	painter
bigger	shopper	runner	older	jumper	faster	baker

Proofreading

Proofread the questions below. Use proofreading marks to correct four spelling mistakes, one capitalization mistake, and one punctuation mistake.

Proofreading Marks

○ spell correctly

≡ capitalize

? add question mark

What I Want to Know

1. Does a newspaper writter have to be a good speller?

2. What does a teacher's hepler do

3. Does a firefighter have to run fastur than most other people?

4. how early does a bakker have to get up?

Dictionary Skills

ABC Order

Some of the **er** words in this lesson are describing words. To find an **er** describing word in a dictionary, look for the base word. For example, to find the word **bigger**, look for **big**.

Write these words in ABC order. Then find each word in a dictionary. Write its page number.

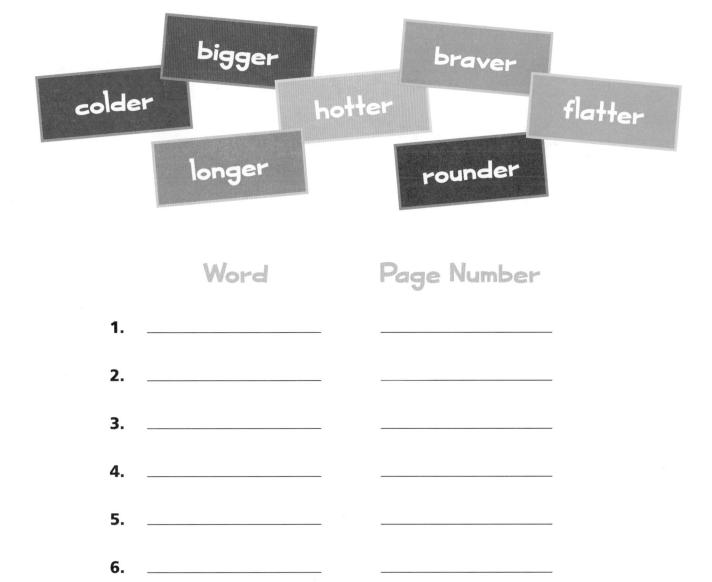

	Word	Page Number
1.		
2.		
3.		
4.		
5.		
6.		
7.		

unit 6 Review
Lessons 26-30

---

out
around
town
flower

The Vowel Sound in out

Write the spelling word for each meaning.

1. the part of a plant that blooms _____

2. not in _____

3. a large village _____

4. in a circle _____

---

saw
talk
small
off

The Vowel Sound in saw

Write the spelling word that completes each sentence.

5. You must _____ softly in a library.

6. Please turn _____ the stove.

7. These shoes are too _____ for me.

8. We _____ two beavers in the pond.

---

orange
store
floor
four

The Vowel Sound in for

Write the spelling word that belongs in each group.

9. two, three, _____

10. wall, ceiling, _____

11. red, yellow, _____

12. shop, market, _____

The Vowel Sound in jar

father
dark
party
are

Write the spelling word for each clue.

13. This man has a child. _____

14. This word goes with **am** and **is**. _____

15. If it is not light outside, it is this. _____

16. You have this on your birthday. _____

Words with er

longer
older
bigger
writer

Write the spelling word that completes each sentence and rhymes with the underlined word.

17. A snake is _____ and stronger than a worm.

18. A _____ needs light that is brighter than candle light.

19. Please hand me the _____ folder.

20. The _____ digger found the gold.

commonly misspelled words

about	family	name	their
above	favorite	nice	then
across	friend	now	there
again	friends	once	they
a lot	get	one	though
am	getting	our	time
and	girl	out	today
another	goes	outside	too
are	guess	party	two
because	have	people	upon
been	hear	play	very
before	her	please	want
beginning	here	pretty	was
bought	him	read	went
boy	his	really	were
buy	house	right	when
can	in	said	where
came	into	saw	white
children	know	scared	with
color	like	school	would
come	little	sent	write
didn't	made	some	writing
does	make	store	wrote
don't	me	swimming	your
every	my	teacher	you're

spelling Table

Consonants

Sound	Example Words	Spellings
b	big	b
ch	child, catch	ch tch
d	day, add	d dd
f	fast, off	f ff
g	get, egg	g gg
h	hand, who	h wh
j	jog, sponge	j g
k	can, keep, school, sick	c k ch ck
ks	six	x
kw	quit	qu
l	look, all	l ll
m	made, swimming, numb	m mm mb
n	not, running, knock	n nn kn
ng	thank, ring	n ng
p	pet, dropped	p pp
r	run, writer	wr
s	sat, dress, city	s ss c
sh	she	sh
t	ten, matter	t tt
th	that, thing	th
v	have, of	v f
w	went, whale, one	w wh o
y	you	y
z	zoo, blizzard, says	z zz s

Vowels

Sound	Example Words	Spellings
short a	cat, have	a a_e
long a	baby, take, play, nail, eight, they	a a_e ay ai eigh ey
ah	father, star	a
short e	red, tread, many, said, says	e ea a ai ay
long e	he, eat, tree, people, belief, very	e ea ee eo ie y
short i	is, give	i i_e
long i	find, ride, pie, high my, eye	i i_e ie igh y eye
short o	on, want	o a
long o	so, nose, road, boulder, snow	o o_e oa ou ow
oi	boy	oy
aw	off, call, haul, saw	o a au aw
o	corn, store, door, four	o o_e oo ou
long oo	zoo, blue, new, do, you	oo ue ew o ou
short oo	good, could, pull	oo ou u
ow	out, owl	ou ow
short u	run, brother	u o

Answer Key

Page 8
1. an, after, and, am, add
2. van, flat, hand, cat, has, than, man

Page 9
1. cat
2. hand
3. add
4. after
5. man
6. an
7. than
8. has
9. am
10. flat
11. and

Page 10
Spell correctly: man, hand, an, am
Capitalize: We
Add period after: tiger

Page 11
1. My cat is stuck in a tree.
2. A man comes to help.
3. He has a ladder.
4. She jumps down and runs home.

Page 12
1. ask
2. catch, fast, matter, (have), land, that, back, last, thank, sang, black

Page 13
1. sang
2. land
3. black
4. catch
5. fast
6. have
7. ask
8. thank
9. matter
10. back
11. that

Page 14
Spell correctly: catch, That, Last, ask
Capitalize: My
Add period after: it (at the end of the fifth sentence)

Page 15
1. A camel can carry people on its back.
2. Some camels have one hump.
3. Camels can run fast.
4. They run across dry land.

Page 16
1. ten, when, bed, shelf, jet, yes, went, kept, next, end
2. says
3. said

Page 17
1. bed
2. shelf
3. when
4. jet
5. end
6. next
7. said
8. kept
9. ten
10. yes
11. says

Page 18
Spell correctly: went, end, said, next
Capitalize: Ted
Add period after: trip

Page 19
1. My friend has ten cats.
2. They hid under the bed.
3. They sat on a shelf.
4. They played with a toy Jet.

Page 20
1. best, well, seven, dress, desk, rest, bell, send, help, egg
2. any, many

Page 21
1. seven
2. many
3. desk
4. best
5. any
6. well
7. egg
8. bell
9. send
10. rest
11. dress

Page 22
Spell correctly: many, seven, any, best
Capitalize: That
Add question mark after: turtles

Page 23
1. city
2. black
3. whale
4. school
5. mouse
6. snail

Page 24
1. had, him, you, our, the, her
2. class, children, boys, girls, them, child

Page 25
1. them
2. her
3. the
4. class
5. children
6. child
7. our
8. had
9. boys
10. you
11. him

Page 26
Spell correctly: class, children, girls, Our
Capitalize: When
Add period after: me

Page 27
These missing letters should be written: b, e, g, h, l, o, r, s, w, z
1. boys
2. class
3. girls
4. him
5. them
6. you

Page 28
1. hand
2. am
3. after
4. than
5. that
6. ask
7. have
8. catch

Page 29
9. says
10. kept
11. when
12. said
13. egg
14. many
15. any
16. seven
17. you
18. girls
19. children
20. our

Page 30
1. big, six, his, hid
2. ship, will, fill, hill, this, wind, pick
3. trick

Page 31
1. hill
2. ship
3. trick
4. six
5. wind
6. fill
7. his
8. big
9. pick
10. this
11. will

Page 32
Spell correctly: six, pick, wind, fill
Capitalize: It (the first word in the fourth sentence)
Add period after: six

Page 33
1. How big is a blue whale?
2. Is it as large as a ship?
3. What does this animal eat?
4. Can you see his tail?

Page 34
1. ring, (give), fish, wish, with, (live), swim
2. think, thing, bring
3. spring, sister

Page 35
1. spring
2. fish
3. ring
4. think
5. bring
6. wish
7. give
8. sister
9. thing
10. swim
11. with

Page 36
Spell correctly: think, Bring, with, thing
Capitalize: It (in the last sentence)
Add question mark after: vegetables

Page 37
1. sister
2. give
3. ring
4. live
5. spring
6. thing
7. wish

Page 38
1. hot, dot, not, block, job, jog, top, on, hop, got
2. what, was

Page 39
1. jog
2. hot
3. hop
4. dot
5. job
6. block
7. got
8. on
9. not
10. what
11. was

Page 40
Spell correctly: not, on, block, what
Capitalize: Do
Add period after: home

Page 41
1. Corey Jones wanted to go for a jog.
2. He and I ran around the block.
3. I saw Rusty hop on the porch.
4. She got the paper.
5. Rusty was running fast.

Page 42
1. box, rock, spot, drop, clock, stop, chop, ox, pond, shop
2. wash, want

Page 43
1. clock
2. want
3. stop
4. chop
5. ox
6. pond
7. wash
8. shop
9. spot
10. drop
11. rock

Page 44
Spell correctly: wash, box, shop, clock
Capitalize: I (would like a box of cereal)
Add question mark after: nuts

Page 45
1. ox; cattle
2. pond; water
3. spot; small
4. rock; solid

Page 46
1. eggs, ships, vans, cats, hands, jobs, jets, bells, desks, backs
2. dresses
3. men

Page 47
1. dresses
2. bells
3. ships
4. eggs
5. vans
6. jobs
7. backs
8. men
9. hands
10. jets
11. desks

Page 48
Spell correctly: jobs, men, vans, backs
Capitalize: They're
Add period after: cages

Page 49
1. bells; bell; page number will vary.
2. eggs; egg; page number will vary.
3. jets; jet; page number will vary.

Page 50
1. pick
2. six
3. will
4. this
5. give
6. sister
7. think
8. live

Page 51
9. block
10. was
11. what
12. not
13. want
14. clock
15. stop
16. wash
17. hands
18. desks
19. men
20. dresses

Page 52
1. sun, under, club, run, bug, mud, summer, bus, us, up, cut, but
2. from, of

Page 53
1. up
2. under
3. from
4. us
5. summer
6. but
7. run
8. bus
9. sun
10. cut
11. club

12. bug
13. mud

Page 54
Spell correctly: up,
　bug, sun, under
Capitalize: You (can sit
　in the sun)
Add period after: tree

Page 55
1. run
2. cut
3. jump
4. shut
5. dug

Page 56
1. just, jump, such,
　skunk, much, truck,
　lunch, fun
2. brother, (come), (love),
　mother, (one), other

Page 57
1. fun
2. much
3. just
4. such
5. love
6. other
7. come
8. jump
9. brother
10. mother
11. lunch
12. one
13. truck

Page 58
Spell correctly: mother,
　just, truck, lunch
Capitalize: I (put him
　in our garage)
Add question mark
　after: afternoon

Page 59
1. Frog contests are fun!
2. Look at the frog my
　brother has!
3. That frog can jump
　very high!
4. It can jump more
　than ten feet!

Page 60
1. game, came, bake,
　whale, ate, name,
　brave, gave
2. today, play, say,
　stay, maybe
3. baby

Page 61
1. bake
2. brave
3. say
4. maybe
5. stay
6. play

7. today
8. game
9. gave
10. name
11. ate
12. baby
13. came

Page 62
Spell correctly: came,
　game, play, Today
Capitalize: Tate
Add period after: end

Page 63
1. bake
2. bed
3. big
4. blame
5. box
6. brave

Page 64
1. chain, gain, tail, paint,
　nail, pail, snail, rain,
　wait, mail, train, sail
2. eight
3. they

Page 65
1. rain
2. train
3. nail
4. gain
5. paint
6. snail
7. they
8. chain
9. sail
10. pail
11. eight
12. wait
13. tail

Page 66
Spell correctly: wait,
　train, snail, eight
Capitalize: Are
Add question mark
　after: train

Page 67
1. 2
2. 1
3. 1
4. 2
5. 2

Page 68
1. tricked, ended,
　wished, handed,
　thanked, asked,
　fished
2. helping, wishing,
　fishing, dressing,
　picking, thinking,
　catching

Page 69
1. asked
2. ended

3. helping
4. catching
5. fished
6. thanked
7. wished
8. fishing
9. picking
10. dressing
11. tricked
12. wishing
13. thinking

Page 70
Spell correctly:
　thanked, tricked,
　wished, fishing
Capitalize: He (wished
　that he had won)
Add period after: ribbon

Page 71
1. helped
2. helping
3. asked
4. asking
5. tricked
6. tricking

Page 72
1. under
2. of
3. cut
4. from
5. come
6. just
7. much
8. other

Page 73
9. baby
10. say
11. gave
12. maybe
13. eight
14. train
15. wait
16. they
17. thinking
18. asked
19. thanked
20. helping

Page 74
1. we, he, she, being
2. see, green, keep, feet,
　bees, street, week,
　three
3. these
4. people

Page 75
1. bees
2. green
3. feet
4. he
5. week
6. she
7. these
8. we
9. see
10. people

11. street
12. being
13. keep

Page 76
Spell correctly: people,
　street, bees, keep
Capitalize: Soon
Add period after: stung

Page 77
1. I have been to Ohio
　three times.
2. My grandfather is in
　Dallas this week.
3. These trees grow all
　over Maine.
4. We went to see my
　aunt in Seattle.

Page 78
1. clean, please, leap,
　peach, eat, heat,
　dream, mean
2. happy, very, funny,
　city, puppy, penny

Page 79
1. happy
2. clean
3. mean
4. heat
5. city
6. please
7. peach
8. leap
9. funny
10. eat
11. puppy
12. penny
13. dream

Page 80
Spell correctly: very,
　penny, clean, city
Capitalize: Peru
Add period after: week

Page 81
1. eat
2. happy
3. leap
Guide words will vary.

Page 82
1. like, ice, bike, side,
　nine, write, mine, ride,
　white, hide, inside,
　five
2. find
3. eye

Page 83
1. bike
2. like
3. ride
4. white
5. write
6. inside
7. find
8. eye

9. hide
10. nine
11. side
12. ice
13. mine

Page 84
Spell correctly: like, ice,
　white, inside
Capitalize: A (team of
　white dogs pulled us)
Add period after: miles

Page 85
1. hide
2. hid
3. wrote
4. write
5. like
6. liked

Page 86
1. lion, tiny, tiger
2. sky, cry, why,
　by, try, my, fly
3. pie, tie, lie
4. high

Page 87
1. high
2. cry
3. tiny
4. lie
5. my
6. pie
7. tie
8. lion
9. try
10. why
11. sky
12. tiger
13. by

Page 88
Spell correctly: sky,
　tiny, fly, try
Capitalize: March
Add period after: enough

Page 89
1. 3
2. 2
3. 1
4. 3
5. 1

Page 90
1. dropped, spotted,
　hopped, jogged,
　shopped, stopped,
　dotted
2. dropping, cutting,
　stopping, jogging,
　running, hopping,
　shopping

Page 91
1. hopped
2. jogging
3. dotted
4. stopped

5. shopped
6. dropped
7. dropping
8. jogged
9. stopping
10. hopping
11. running
12. spotted
13. shopping

Page 92
Spell correctly: jogging,
　jogged, stopping,
　running
Capitalize: There
Add question mark
　after: fun

Page 93
1. shopping
2. shopped
3. hopping
4. hopped
5. stopped
6. stopping

Page 94
1. being
2. week
3. street
4. people
5. clean
6. very
7. funny
8. please
9. write
10. eye
11. find
12. white

Page 95
13. tie
14. tiny
15. why
16. high
17. hopping
18. stopped
19. dropped
20. running

Page 96
1. go, no, so
2. home, rope, nose,
　hope, stone,
　hole, joke
3. yellow, grow,
　know, snow

Page 97
1. snow
2. yellow
3. nose
4. no
5. rope
6. home
7. hole
8. hope
9. stone
10. joke
11. grow
12. so
13. go

Page 98
Spell correctly: go, rope, snow, stone
Capitalize: Last
Add question mark after: trip

Page 99
1. whole
2. hole
3. know
4. no
5. sew
6. so
7. so

Page 100
1. cold, gold, old, sold, open, over, roll, most, hold, told
2. road, goat, coat, boat

Page 101
1. sold
2. over
3. coat
4. cold
5. open
6. boat
7. told
8. gold
9. road
10. goat
11. hold
12. old
13. most

Page 102
Spell correctly: most, gold, coat, cold
Capitalize: Our
Add period after: snow

Page 103
1. road
2. told
3. roll
4. gold
5. over
6. open
7. old
8. cold

Page 104
1. book, look, cook, stood, cookies, good, foot, took
2. could, would, should
3. put, pull, full

Page 105
1. cookies
2. would
3. cook
4. put
5. book
6. could
7. stood
8. should
9. look

10. pull
11. took
12. full
13. good

Page 106
Spell correctly: Would, full, look, cook
Capitalize: Oak
Add period after: cookies

Page 107
1. Mr. Roy Gray
2. 1631 Elm Rd.
3. Mrs. Jean Ryan
4. 402 Bank St.
5. Mr. Yoshi Ono
6. 6800 Burnet Rd.
7. Mrs. Deana Reyna
8. 509 State St.
9. Mr. Jackson Palmer

Page 108
1. zoo, too, room, food, school, tooth, soon, moon
2. blue
3. new
4. to, do, who, two

Page 109
1. moon
2. who
3. zoo
4. food
5. soon
6. tooth
7. room
8. blue
9. to
10. new
11. do
12. too
13. two

Page 110
Spell correctly: too, do, zoo, soon
Capitalize: Dad
Add period after: zoo

Page 111
1. zoo
2. tooth
3. room
4. moon

Page 112
1. named, biked, hoped, liked, lived, baked, loved
2. joking, baking, living, giving, riding, writing, having

Page 113
1. biked
2. writing
3. baking

4. joking
5. hoped
6. loved
7. named
8. baked
9. lived
10. giving
11. having
12. living
13. riding

Page 114
Spell correctly: baked, hoped, riding, joking
Capitalize: Mr.
Add question mark after: joking

Page 115
1. live
2. give
3. have
4. write
5. love
6. bike
7. name
8. like
Page numbers will vary.

Page 116
1. know
2. yellow
3. no
4. home
5. coat
6. open
7. cold
8. over

Page 117
9. book
10. would
11. pull
12. put
13. could
14. tooth
15. blue
16. two
17. new
18. writing
19. liked
20. riding

Page 118
1. out, found, sound, mouse, round, around, house
2. town, now, flower, owl, how, cow, clown

Page 119
1. flower
2. round
3. around
4. out
5. found
6. clown
7. sound
8. house
9. how

10. owl
11. town
12. mouse
13. now

Page 120
Spell correctly: town, around, found, house
Capitalize: Then
Add question mark after: draw

Page 121
1. The dog was afraid of the sound.
2. The boys were glad to see the owl.
3. The child was picking a flower.
4. How many stores were in that town?
5. A mouse was hiding in my shoe.

Page 122
1. saw, draw
2. talk, call, ball, all, small, walk
3. song, dog, frog, off, lost, long

Page 123
1. dog
2. call
3. frog
4. walk
5. talk
6. draw
7. saw
8. song
9. small
10. lost
11. long
12. off
13. all

Page 124
Spell correctly: small, long, call, ball
Capitalize: He (has long black hair).
Add period after: hair

Page 125
1. o
2. ete
3. o
4. i
5. o
6. k

Page 126
1. for, corn, or, story, short, snore, more, horse, storm, orange, store
2. door, floor
3. four

Page 127
1. corn
2. storm
3. store
4. short
5. four
6. horse
7. more
8. for
9. or
10. orange
11. snore
12. door
13. floor

Page 128
Spell correctly: store, corn, orange, short
Capitalize: We (also have special feeding dishes)
Add period after: dish

Page 129
1. Snow has fallen for four days and nights.
2. Watch out for the snow above that door!
3. Do you think we will get more snow?

Page 130
1. father
2. jar, car, party, barn, arm, mark, farmer, star, are, dark, farm, far, art

Page 131
1. farmer
2. art
3. arm
4. jar
5. are
6. farm
7. father
8. dark
9. far
10. party
11. mark
12. star
13. barn

Page 132
Spell correctly: party, dark, barn, arm
Capitalize: Every
Add question mark after: say

Page 133
1. star; 2
2. mark; 1
3. star; 1
4. mark; 2
5. star; 1
6. mark; 1

Page 134
1. colder, helper, older, longer, jumper, faster, painter
2. bigger, shopper, runner, flatter
3. braver, writer, baker

Page 135
1. shopper
2. helper
3. writer
4. braver
5. runner
6. flatter
7. jumper
8. painter
9. older
10. faster
11. longer
12. bigger
13. colder

Page 136
Spell correctly: writer, helper, faster, baker
Capitalize: How
Add question mark after: do

Page 137
1. bigger
2. braver
3. colder
4. flatter
5. hotter
6. longer
7. rounder
Page numbers will vary.

Page 138
1. flower
2. out
3. town
4. around
5. talk
6. off
7. small
8. saw
9. four
10. floor
11. orange
12. store

Page 139
13. father
14. are
15. dark
16. party
17. longer
18. writer
19. older
20. bigger

▼ "Coyote melon," actually an inedible gourd,
grows amid the cholla cactus gardens of Joshua
Tree National Monument. LARRY ULRICH

Also available in the California Geographic Series

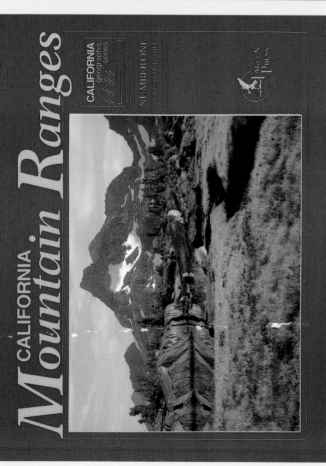

California State Parks
by Kim Heacox

Whether you're interested in scenery, science, recreation, or history, you'll find it in *California State Parks*, Book Two of the California Geographic Series. With one hundred twenty-two outstanding color photographs, this is a journey of discovery through the state park system that you won't want to miss. A special eighteen-page guide highlights the attractions and facilities available in each park to make planning your vacation easy.

128 pages, 11" x 8½", $14.95 softcover, $24.95 hardcover

California Mountain Ranges
by Russell B. Hill

Here is a book to match California's mountains. Explore every range in the state with a knowledgeable and interesting text and vivid color photography that will make you wish you were there. Book One of the California Geographic Series, *California Mountain Ranges* will educate and enchant outdoor enthusiasts, mountaineers, and weekend travelers alike

120 pages, 11" x 8 1/2", $14.95 softcover, $24.95 hardcover

California Wildlife, Book Four
by Bernard Shanks

Falcon Press presents the most complete roundup ever of the wildlife in California in Book Four of the California Geographic Series. Never before have the state's fascinating creatures been so beautifully captured in exquisite full-color photos and an authoritative yet easy-to-read text.

128 pages, 11" x 8½", $14.95 softcover

To order:

California Mountain Ranges, California State Parks, California Deserts, California Wildlife

Call toll-free 1-800-582-2665 to order with Visa or Mastercard. Or send a check or money order and include $2.50 postage and handling for each book to Falcon Press, P.O. Box 1718, Helena, MT 59624. (OUR GUARANTEE: If you are dissatisfied with any book obtained from Falcon Press, simply return your purchase for a full refund.)